REMAKE it HOME

REMAKE it HOME

THE ESSENTIAL GUIDE TO RESOURCEFUL LIVING

Henrietta Thompson | Illustrations by Neal Whittington

Universe

To Olivia, for pun times and inspiration.

First published in the United States of America in 2009 by
UNIVERSE PUBLISHING
A Division of Rizzoli International Publications, Inc.
300 Park Avenue South
New York, NY 10010
www.rizzoliusa.com

Originally published in the United Kingdom in 2009 by
Thames & Hudson Ltd
181A High Holborn
London WC1V 7QX
thamesandhudson.com

2009 2010 2011 2012 / 10 9 8 7 6 5 4 3 2 1

ISBN: 978-0-7893-2056-8

Library of Congress Control Number: 2009902757

Designed by EMMI / www.emmi.co.uk
Cover designed by Linda Pricci
Cover images: Photo Tim Bjørn, www.fritzhansen.com

Printed and bound in China

This book is printed on Cyclus Offset paper, which is
100% recycled stock, manufactured using only post-
consumer de-inked waste.

Please note: The tips and instructions in this book
are intended as inspiration. The nature of this way of
working means that the materials, tools, and outcomes
of every project are likely to differ hugely depending on
your individual skill levels and the materials you have
on hand, and all projects involve some degree of risk.
Although the author has made every effort to ensure
that the advice in this book is correct, it is provided
for general information only. Always read any relevant
manuals or instructions before using tools and chemicals
and follow the manufacturer's safety recommendations.
Before working with electrical or plumbing devices, you
should consult a qualified professional, and always turn
the power or water off at the mains. The techniques
suggested in the book should not be used by anyone
under eighteen years of age. The author and the
publisher accept no liability for any loss, damage, or
injury arising as a consequence of the advice contained
in this book.

747
THO
2009

Contents

Introduction

Design is the Daddy

This book exists at the intersection of design and necessity, bringing together what the world has learned about being resourceful in a way that is relevant to modern life. In past generations it was *de rigeur* to make the most of what you had; in our own time, environmental and economic change is reviving the "Make Do and Mend" ethos in creative and unexpected ways. This book is not intended to teach you how to tan your legs with tea bags, but to inspire you to be resourceful in making your home a stylish and practical place to live. From the wisdom of bygone days to innovative ideas from contemporary artists, designers and communities around the world, we have everything we need — if only we know where to look.

Mezzadro Stool – Achille and Pier Giacomo Castiglioni

Designers have been rummaging in bins for as long as there have been bins to rummage in. One of the earliest examples was Achille and Pier Giacomo Castiglioni's 1957 Mezzadro Stool, which was constructed from a tractor seat. Their use of industrial components had nothing to do with lean times, nor was it an attempt to be environmentally sound. Instead the Castiglionis were proposing a new way of looking at how and by whom objects and furniture were made, and what constituted a valid raw material.

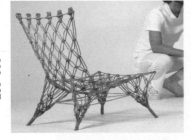

Cappillini Knotted Chair – Marcel Wanders for Droog

Although remaking, recycling and reusing waste is often portrayed as a new trend in contemporary design, "appropriation" is in fact a lasting aesthetic movement that spans at least half a century. As early as 1917 Marcel Duchamp was making art from mass-produced ceramic urinals – just one of many "Readymades" he built throughout his career. Picasso took the appropriation bull by the horns too, with a bovine-inspired sculpture made from a bicycle seat and handlebars in 1943. Around the same time, Joseph Cornell's fascination with thrift made him one of America's most well-respected twentieth-century artists and sculptors. Heavily influenced by the Surrealists, the New York artist is best known for his boxed assemblages created from found objects.

The idea has also infiltrated the world of architecture, albeit under a slightly different guise. The term "adhocism" was coined by theorist Charles Jencks in 1968 to describe "using an available system or dealing with an existing situation in a new way to solve a problem quickly and efficiently." Adhocism, according to Jencks, was "a method of creation relying particularly on resources which are ready to hand." Democratic by design, items made in an ad-hoc manner were rarely intended for mass production, and indeed could be recreated by anyone with similar tools at their disposal.

When post-industrial waste became the material of choice for a whole troop of designer punks in the 1980s, the key driver behind what was by then a fledgling movement had evolved. Reappropriating industrial waste and mass-produced items was the design equivalent of the anarchic punk-rock spirit that was taking hold of the music scene. It was about rebellion.

Ron Arad became a champion of post-industrial salvage chic in the early 1980s with a number high-profile experimental pieces using bits of scaffolding and old car seats, and opened the One Off Gallery on London's Neal Street in 1983. A space where other like-minded creatives could exhibit and sell their work, the gallery played host to the likes of Tom Dixon, with his Creative Salvage work, and Danny Lane, whose furniture made from layers of broken glass incited a rash of media attention.

The work at the gallery was characteristically rough; welded metal from railings, manhole covers and other "street" finds featured heavily. If the movement represented design's answer to punk rock, then Dixon's group Creative Salvage, established in 1984 with Mark Brazier-Jones and Nick Jones, was akin to the Sex Pistols. Creative Salvage stood in direct opposition to "expensive, anonymous, mass produced hi-tech products", instead offering "a more decorative, human approach" via "the recycling of scrap". Dixon himself was not a trained designer or artist, and so the results were deemed all the more democratic, edgy and controversial.

As the movement gained momentum, its exclusive and unique one-off pieces began to fetch extremely high prices. The anti-bourgeois, anti-consumerist ethic started to fade, and Arad and Dixon moved on to other experiments, although neither designer would forget his recycled roots. In 2000, Dixon penned a book called *Rethink*, promoting reuse and recycling in design from a practical, rather than fashionable standpoint.

The wave might have broken but it was swiftly followed by another, and in the 1990s, the appropriation movement was to gain new ground. Thanks in no small part to the Castiglioni brothers, still evolving their original ideas in pieces such as the highly acclaimed Fix bench for De Padova, a new ironic undertone would inspire British designer Jasper Morrison to take up the "readymade" cause. Morrison was just beginning his career and had no way of accessing factory resources. Readymades (for example, the terracotta pots he used for the base of a table that would later be manufactured by Cappellini) provided a convenient shortcut.

Following on from Morrison, the simplicity, economy, universality and (sometimes) elegance of remaking and reappropriating objects and furniture inspired an entire generation of designers. In 1992 design historian Renny Ramakers staged a small show of furniture constructed by young Dutch designers using low-cost industrial materials and found objects, second hand dresser drawers and driftwood. The exhibition toured the Netherlands and Belgium, and the pieces – by designers such as Jan Konings and Jurgen Bey, Piet Hein Eek and

Tree Trunk Bench – Jurgen Bey for Droog

Set Up Shades – Marcel Wanders for Droog

Tejo Remy – were widely acclaimed, despite being slow to sell. The consensus was that Ramakers had discovered a new approach to design. Ramakers went on to collaborate with Gijs Bakker, a product designer and professor at the Design Academy in Eindhoven. Together they established Droog Design the following year, producing Marcel Wanders's Set Up Shades and a bathmat by Hella Jongerius, among other pieces. Displaying the same rebellious style that characterized the work of Creative Salvage, the humour behind the Droog collections made them instant hits. Meanwhile, in the US, Constantine and Lauryn Boym were building up their reputation with initiatives such as Searstyle – a collection of furniture rethinking

Searstyle – Constantine and Lauryn Boym

old Sears products – and a number of other readymades. The refreshing humour of the Boyms' work was in a similar spirit to that of British designer Michael Marriott, another pioneer of appropriation, who famously built a chest of drawers using sardine tins in order to celebrate the design of the packaging. When he saw lampshade potential in an upturned yellow bucket, it had nothing to do with recycling or using "found" objects; he

simply liked the idea of putting a hole for the light fitting in the bottom of the pail.

Dutch designer Jurgen Bey took a different approach to appropriation, wrapping up old objects in new technology. His Kokon furniture range in 1999 for Droog saw a series of old chairs and tables cocooned in spun PVC – their original forms clearly visible and recognisable, but protected and sealed as if in a time capsule.

Humour and nostalgia couldn't have been further from Tord Boontje's mind when he launched his Rough and Ready collection of utilitarian furniture made from found wood and recycled materials in 1994. Boontje, who had just graduated from design school, was questioning the relevance of high design in a world where vast numbers of people still depended on this kind of makeshift furniture. Incredibly poor quality – and intentionally so – the controversial designs hit a nerve when they were exhibited. Boontje made his blueprints freely available to anyone who wanted to build the pieces, and tens of thousands were distributed.

In the contemporary art world, meanwhile, artists continue to turn to salvaged materials in their work. Artist Leo Fitzmaurice has been described as "an urban Andy Goldsworthy"; he prefers the term "detourist". In one of his best known projects, between 2004 and 2006 Fitzmaurice traveled between Berlin, London, Shanghai, Stavanger, Zurich and his home city of Liverpool, creating temporary public artworks by rearranging found materials such as catalogues, flyers, or cardboard. Another project, "Craterform", saw Fitzmaurice take the well-known British Argos shopping catalogue and tear holes in every page to evoke a black hole in catalogue commerce.

Appropriation is an answer to many serious issues faced by the world, and designers – the world's self-appointed problem solvers – have found many a reason to turn to it in their work. Environmental concerns and economic constraints are making appropriation an increasingly attractive path for young designers, and many examples of their work are shown on the following pages.

Whatever the motivation, however, one aspect of the appropriation movement is certain: it might slow down but it will never cease completely. Throughout the decades, encompassing art, design, architecture and craft alike, appropriation is timeless by definition.

Necessity is the Mother

Brainstorming sessions, long walks in nature, mind-altering drugs – there are many options available if you're looking to boost your creativity. Some are more effective than others, but a quick look through world history shows that hard times are what really make fresh ideas flow.

We know that when the going gets tough, the tough get going; desperate times call for desperate measures; everything is worth something to somebody and whatever doesn't kill you makes you stronger. *Per aspera ad astra*, as the philospher Seneca put it: through hardship, to the stars.

Some of the best remaking ideas are products of the climate of thrift and self-reliance that flourished during the Great Depression of the 1930s, a time when people would not only mend holes in socks rather than throw them out (that went without saying) but also reinforce the stitching as a precaution. In modern times, faced

with a high cost of living, Japanese city-dwellers trade *urawaza* – tips for household frugality– on national television shows. To combat food and electricity shortages in sub-Saharan Africa, a Nigerian teacher invented a refrigerator using only two pots and some wet sand. Necessity, as another saying goes, is the mother of invention.

In times of war and political upheaval the struggle for survival has triggered an extraordinary flowering of creativity around the world. Textile and fuel rationing during the Second World War encouraged European, American and Australian housewives to cook dinners in hay boxes and make stockings out of parachute silk. The oft-repeated motto of militant remakers, "Make Do & Mend", comes from government pamphlets of this era, as do some of the tips in this book.

Contemporary Russian artist Vladimir Arkhipov made a book and an exhibition about similar innovations made by ordinary Russians when they were denied access to manufactured goods during the collapse of the Soviet Union. (*Home Made*, Fuel, 2006). The more than 100 items in Arkhipov's collection include a wastepaper basket fashioned from an old

Kokon furniture – Jurgen Bey for Droog

hay basket, a thread spooler made from a plastic water bottle and a few straws, and a bath plug carved from the rubber heel of an old shoe with a fork stuck in it for a handle. The artist collectively terms these handmade creations "thingamyjigs". Having grown up in a house where the television aerial was constructed from unwanted forks, Arkhipov sees such ingenious and resourceful solutions as integral to Soviet culture. However during his years of research he has also discovered that people have taken matters into their own hands in this way for centuries, all around the world. A renowned archaeologist in Berlin was dumbfounded by Arkhipov's collection as some of the objects resembled ancient Egyptian items whose purposes he had been puzzling over for years.

Detourist – Leo Fitzmaurice

A personal economic crisis can be as a potent a catalyst for invention as a global depression – as one Jose Avila found out. When the computer programmer moved from California to Arizona in 2005, he found himself in a bit of a fix: still paying rent on his old apartment in California, he had little money and no furniture. What he did have, however, were some old FedEx boxes and a handy way with a knife. Avila constructed chairs, tables, a bed, shelves, a sofa and a desk from the sturdy boxes, then set up a website to tell the world. When Fedexfurniture.com went live it was an instant hit, and his message, "it's OK to be ghetto", was spread around the world. Of course the world already knew this – many cultural traditions that we take for granted have their roots in reappropriation.

Every culture seems to have a signature item that can be adapted for any situation. As explained by author Douglas Adams in his *Hitchhiker's Guide to the Galaxy*, a humble towel could be the most useful item for any interstellar traveller: you can wave it in emergencies, use it to sail a mini raft down the river Moth, or wrap it around you for warmth as you bound across the cold moons of Jaglan Beta. For a pioneer American family in the 1880s, meanwhile, the equivalent to Adams's towel might be a handsewn quilt, which would see many different uses in its lifetime and was itself made from recycled clothing. As the family packed for the long trek west, the quilt could be wrapped around breakable items in a trunk; en route, it could be used as travel bedding, a seat-cushion or to cover cracks in the wagon when winds rose up on the planes bringing with them clouds of choking dust. In a few reported cases, quilts were hung on the exposed side of a wagon during Indian attacks to offer protection from arrows. While the family finally reached their destination, the hardy quilts would be used to cover windows and doors or hung for partitions in rudimentary one-room cabins.

The Japanese equivalent to the pioneer American quilt might be the *furoshiki* cloth, a type of traditional wrapping cloth that was once used to transport clothes, gifts and other goods, and could even be used for clothing. *Furoshiki* means "bath spread", a name coined during a time when the technique was used to bundle clothes at the public baths. Essentially, *furoshiki* is a practical form of origami using textiles instead of paper. The cloth can be reused as necessary, and the uses for the technique are seemingly endless. Largely used in modern Japan to wrap and transport bento boxes, the cloths then double as a table mat for the lunch while its being eaten. An especially attractive piece of cloth might make a nice alternative when wrapping up a present, while an old sheet might still make a perfectly serviceable laundry bag. Although the use of *furoshiki* declined after the Second World War due to the proliferation of the plastic shopping bag, as environmental consciousness has intensified in recent decades, the technique has experienced a revival.

In modern society we have found a way to nurture an inventive streak even at times when necessity is nowhere in sight. Ikea Hacking is "post-purchase product alteration" for a generation keen to adapt the commercial offerings of the low-cost flat-packed furniture manufacturer to better suit its various whims. The Swedish homewares giant does not just provide cheap chairs, cute cutlery and starter-home solutions for the masses, but is the unwitting purveyor of a whole array of raw materials with which it is possible to build almost any new product you can think of, and which are far cheaper than what is available at the hardware store. The simple, clean designs often incorporate modular and interchangeable parts (that's not to mention the free allen key) making it easy for the potential hacker to get stuck in.

In 2006 Kuala Lumpur-based copywriter Mei Mei Yap established a blog, ikeahacker.blogspot.com in order to distribute the most creative ideas. Very quickly Yap (whose online pseudonym is Jules, after her favourite Ikea chair) found herself at the helm of a growing community of Ikea hackers worldwide. Although the site is not actively endorsed by Ikea, the company wisely did not take issue with the customisation of its products. (Only a few hackers are actively subverting the brand's ethos, with most simply wanting to make items that fit their particular requirements.) So necessity might be the mother of invention, but there's a big Swedish daddy somewhere in the background as well, and the progeny of these two is unstoppable.

As the sun sets on the late 20th-century "throwaway society", these diverse traditions of recycling, reusing and reappropriating are uniting unlikely communities, across the world and across the generations. While in the past such thrifty measures have been associated with times of need, gradually they are being revived by artists, designers and eco-warriors alike, finding fans in more affluent and image-conscious circles.

Detourist – Leo Fitzmaurice

FURNITURE

Beds, chairs, tables, desks, stools, plinths, benches, sofas and garden furniture

-- Totally rubbish --

Many communities – from Barcelona's local barrios to the hills of Tokyo – have an official "large garbage" day, when people leave furniture and other unwanted large items out in the street where they can be snaffled by the neighbours or carted away later by the local authorities later. The frequency of such occasions varies hugely – from once a year to once a week – but it's worth finding out when yours is when moving into a new place, or even for souvenirs when visiting.

-- Strapped for cash --

A person possessed of some good strapping (old belts, luggage straps or otherwise), can construct makeshift furniture from almost anything. Strap magazines and books together into blocks for stools or tables, or duvets, cushions, clothes and rags to make soft seating. (Don't be tempted to substitute duct tape for the straps if you value the materials that you're strapping, or if you intend to undo the straps after a while.)

-- Put your futon it --

Create a useful modular futon from scavenged sofa cushions. Line up the pads and stitch the covers sturdily together at the edges so that the futon won't break apart when it's in use as a mattress, but can be folded up in a hinged fashion and stored easily on a high shelf. It's usually possible to remove the covers of sofa cushions for cleaning, so bear this in mind when sewing them together so as not to obstruct the zips – one way is to make sure the zips all run along one edge rather than facing towards the centre.

-- Hummer time --

Modern military personnel, while serving in far-flung climes, often with only basic accommodation, have become well-versed in the art of makeshift furniture. A recent invention is the "Hummer seat". A simple wooden box is built, into which the car seat from a no longer serviceable vehicle can be placed to make a very comfortable and sturdy chair. Key to making it work is securing the seat-back in place with a bolt to prevent the back from suddenly moving to a reclining position – could be a little embarrassing to endure in front of one's fellow Marines.

Menimal
Magazine Bench
Mexican designer Menimal
(Francisco Cavada Cantú) built
a bench for an exhibition at
DesignWeek Monterrey from
magazines he needed to recycle.
A simple steel structure holds
the journals – which have been
cut into slabs – securely in place.

Design example

Maybe Design
Sitbag
The charmingly named Sitbag
sees Maybe Design reincarnate
hard-shelled suitcases as lounge
chairs using some generous
padding and the addition of
sleek chrome legs. Maybe
Design, which operates out of
both Vienna and Istanbul, is a
multidisciplinary design and
art practice founded in 2004 by
its four partners Erdem Akan,
Bora Akcay, Susanne Akcay
and Bogac Simsir.

Design example

**Martino Gamper
100 Chairs in 100 Days**
Throughout history, designers
and architects have tried
to create the perfect chair.
According to Martino Gamper,
however, there is no such thing.
In an experimental project and
exhibition, Gamper embarked on
a mission to make 100 chairs in
100 days. Between 2 December
2006 and 25 February 2007, using
a stockpile of discarded and
donated chairs, he dismantled
and amalgamated the old
furniture into new configurations.
It was a spontaneous process;
only when deconstructing each
chair would he decide what to
do with it, gaining insight into its
construction and materials as
he went.

Design example
Junktion
Suitcase Furniture
There are a few basic lessons everyone should know to help them travel light through life: firstly, when you're short of a porter, a suitcase on wheels is the only way to go; and secondly, when you're tired of carrying all that weight it's best to have a sit-down. Israeli design group Junktion must have had these maxims in mind when it designed this series of suitcase furniture items – including a trunk on castors and a low seat with a padded cushion.

Design example
Rotor
Manon Table
This table was made using white Carrara marble that once clad the Library of Human Sciences at the Université Libre de Bruxelles. When the building needed a new façade roughly a decade after its construction, Rotor "rescued" some of the waste plates. The support structure for the table is a former workbench from a failed company that once produced aluminium windows.

-- Side orders --

Coffee tables and side tables are two of the easiest items of furniture to construct ad hoc, because they generally need just two elements: a flat surface, and legs or other supports. Ideas for flat surfaces include old doors and windows, drawing boards, trays, mirrors, stiff cardboard, the lid of an old grand piano, and so on. Supports generally need to be available in multiples, but commonly appropriated objects might be breeze blocks, bricks, books, bottles, flowerpots, castors, goldfish bowls or garden gnomes. For single plinth tables, meanwhile, a stray wine barrel is traditional.

-- Knock knock --

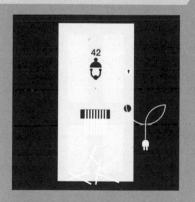

An unwanted door – whether from your own house or someone else's – makes one of the best tabletops. To keep the more door-specific features from getting in the way, try to make the most of them where you can: the hole intended for a doorknob ought to be in the perfect position for threading computer or hi-fi cables, while the letterbox could be adapted into a desk tidy by affixing a small box – or, more fun, a shredder – right underneath it.

-- What a carry on --

Beautifully worn leather? Check. Embossed initials? Check. Elegant design? Check. Vintage suitcases can look so pretty but are rarely practical for actual travel. No wheels? Broken handle? Torn lining? Check check check. But it's still a wrench to thow it out: that suitcase has been places. It exudes a glamorous aura of the golden age of travel. Aside from the obvious option – repurposing it as a storage box – you can always fill it with cushions and make a new bed for the chihuahua. Alternatively legs can easily be affixed to that old attaché to make a useful side table.

Design example
Jasper Morrison
Flowerpot Table

Jasper Morrison, perhaps the ultimate design reductionist, made much use of readymades in the early part of his career – partly as he, like many designers, did not have access to factory resources at that point. One of his first successes – the flowerpot table (designed in 1984 for Cappellini) uses for its base a stack of terracotta flowerpots that Morrison had seen in a Berlin hardware store.

Design example
Jasper Morrison
The Crate

In 2006 Jasper Morrison was commissioned by luxury furniture manufacturer Established & Sons to design a bedside table. After playing with various ideas, he realized that he could not improve upon the old wooden wine crate in which he stored books beside his bed. "Nothing else seemed to do the job as well," said Morrison. He decided to produce a replica of that crate, made from good wood – Douglas fir, rather than splintery pine – with stronger joints. With a price tag to match, the design spurred a surge in the sales of wine by the crate, free bedside table included.

-- Stool crazy after all these years --
Adapt an unwanted vanity stool into a bedside table by removing the upholstered cushion and adding a hard surface, such as a tray or a piece of wood. If you have an old hard-shell briefcase or box file try it out for size too. This way you can also add extra storage space for the wads of cash that won't fit under the mattress, or any other bedside items you might want hidden out of sight.

-- Totally piste --
Wooden furniture that is unwanted, broken or just ugly can be dismantled and the parts reused to make new items, but it is always worth looking further afield for material inspiration. For example an old snowboard, should it become available, can be screwed to a basic box structure to make a bench, while a favourite set of skis might be similarly reappropriated into chairs and tables.

-- Got it nailed --

Scrap wooden boards are relatively easy to come by. Every other skip on the street will hold a treasure trove of old shelving units, floorboards, bed slats and palettes. Armed with a saw, a hammer and some nails it couldn't be easier to reconfigure the planks into tidy side tables. Dovetail joints aren't necessary when you're desperate (the simplest items can be constructed using one plank either side and one on top) but offcuts such as these can provide a great opportunity to hone latent woodworking skills too.

-- Gone to press --

If the ironing board in your house doesn't see a lot of use, or if you simply don't have the storage space for it, repurpose it as a "library table" in the home office for stacks of books and paperwork. The key here is to make the ironing board look as though it's there on purpose, and not as though you just couldn't be bothered to put it away – so keep all crumpled clothes well away. The prettier the board you have to start with the better, naturally, but arranged with a vase of flowers on the stand and perhaps an artfully draped piece of fabric, any old board will do the job nicely.

STEP-BY-STEP

Walk the plank

If you were to plot the evolution of chair design, this would be right up there next to the tree trunk. Invented around about the same time that people learned to make planks from wood, this chair is one of the most basic forms of seating there is, and ancient variations of it can be seen in China, Africa and South America alike. Best for primitive pursuits such as picnicking, it's also the perfect height and angle for videogamers.

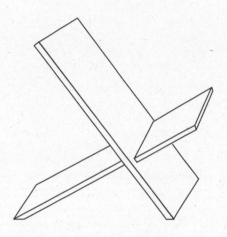

You will need:

_ A long plank of wood
_ A cross-cut saw

_ A drill
_ A keyhole saw
_ Sandpaper and varnish for finishing

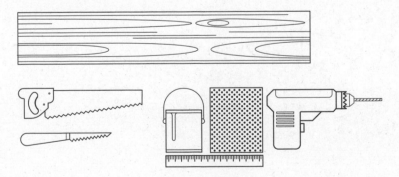

1_ Decide on the dimensions of your chair. The plank you use should be wide enough to accommodate the intended bottom, and strong enough to support the intended sitter's weight. Cut the plank in half.

2_ To make the back leg, cut 5 cm of wood off of the sides of one board starting around 40 cm from one end.

3a Take the second plank and cut a hole in the centre the right size for the back leg to slot into. To do this, place the tapered end of the first board against it and trace around the edge.

3b Drill a starter hole just inside the lines that is large enough to fit the blade of the keyhole saw, and use it to cut out the remainder of the slot.

4_ Fit the two pieces together and have a go at sitting on it. To ensure that the planks will sit neatly at right angles, use a saw to redefine the angles inside the slot.

5_ Finish the planks by sanding them down, carving, painting or decorating as you see fit. And have a seat.

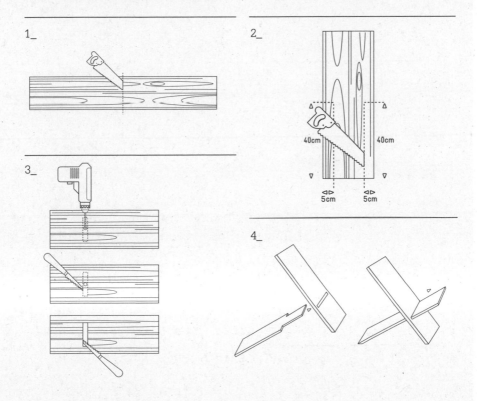

1_

2_

40cm   40cm

◁▷   ◁▷
5cm   5cm

3_

4_

-- Books and crannies --

Old unwanted books and magazines can be stacked together and upholstered to create all sorts of furniture. Covered with padding and fabric, simple blocks are probably the most useful items, as they can be stacked to the perfect height and stored away when they are not in use. As the blocks can end up quite heavy, it is useful to sew a flat handle across the top so they can be picked up and moved easily.

-- Shower scene: soap caddies from fruit crates --

Plastic fruit crates, which can often be picked up from the local grocer or corner store if you ask nicely, make such effective bathroom shelves that it's a wonder they weren't specifically designed with that use in mind. Depending on the space available the crates can easily be cut down to size and mounted on a wall, or stacked inside a homemade frame and used as drawers.

-- Laptop dance --

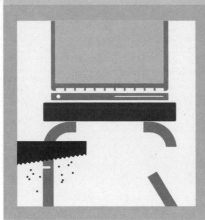

Laptops probably weren't really designed to be used on your actual lap because – as anyone who has ever done so can testify – things get a little toasty on the underside. A pair of hot legs, while generally desirable in other circumstances, is not what you need when you're trying to type that report. Cue the laptop desk – for sale in all good office supplies stores, or, for those who might not want to pay good money for such a thing, easily homemade by lopping the legs off an unwanted stool. The same trick will also leave you with a good tray for serving up a TV dinner.

-- Rim-rim situation --

Bicycle parts are a mainstay in the toolbox of the dedicated remaker, and none more so than the trusty inner tube or wheel rim. The latter, which can be picked up from a local bike dealer or junkyard if you're not a cyclist with spare parts lying around, can be stuffed (sans hub and spokes) to make a low table using sticks or scraps of wood. Level them off at both ends carefully in the style of Uhuru (*see opposite*). Rolled-up magazines or newspapers also work well for stuffing.

Tom Ballhatchet
TV Packaging Stand

Tom Ballhatchet's TV Packaging Stand – a system of packaging that converts into a functional stand once it has protected the TV during transit – attempts to attach a positive narrative to what could be a time of guilt (throwing away great blocks of polystyrene). Ballhatchet sees this concept of contextual reuse of throwaway materials working for things other than TVs – printers, scanners and laptops are some examples.

Uhuru
Stoolen Lite

Following the Shaker maxim that "beauty rests on utility", Uhuru, based in New York, strives to make furniture and products with an acute awareness of materials and craftsmanship. Building each piece by hand in its Brooklyn studio using locally sourced reclaimed and recycled materials, Uhuru has a particular fondness for heart pine, a wood that is virtually extinct due to overharvesting a century ago, but which the designers extract from buildings due for demolition in the city. The Stoolen Lite tables and accompanying chairs are constructed of wood scraps from local workshops, held together in some models by a found bicycle rim.

Design example
Fernando and Humberto Campana
Banquete
Brazilian brothers Fernando
and Humberto Campana are
famous for their ability to
transform anything from a
rubber hose to a fluffy toy into
a collectable and decadent
piece of high design. Having
trained in law and architecture,
respectively, neither brother
ever intended to become a
designer; as a result their work
is always fresh and surprising.
And very Brazilian: primary
materials used in Campana
designs are found objects and
surplus materials from their
home city of São Paulo. By
combining offcuts and factory
rejects with traditional artisanal
techniques and advanced
technologies, the Campana
brothers have established a
distinctively Brazilian approach
to contemporary design. For the
limited-edition Banquete (2003),
stuffed soft toys are piled up on
a simple metal base to make an
armchair that is as utterly cuddly
as it is surreal.

Design example
Fernando and Humberto Campana
Sushi Chair
The Campanas' Sushi Chair
(2002) for Edra uses strips of
colourful plastic and carpet
underlay that have been tightly
rolled and wedged into a basic
frame in one version, while in
another the scraps cascade
out from the centre.

Design example
Tejo Remy
Rag Chair

The Dutch design collective
Droog was formed in 1993
by design historian Renny
Ramakers and designer and
educator Gijs Bakker. Its first
exhibition included Tejo Remy's
Accumulation of Drawers
Without a Cabinet and his Rag
Chair, both designed in 1991 and
made from recycled materials.
The pieces were pioneering at
the time for their do-it-yourself
style and environmental
sensitivity. For the Rag Chair
Remy made a lounger using old
textiles and clothes strapped
together with metal tape.

Design example
Karen Ryan
Custom Made
Frustrated by the waste produced in the pursuit of fashionable interiors, London-based Karen Ryan constructed her Custom Made collection of seating by stacking and amalgamating multiple retired chairs of every style. The result is an ever-expanding range of fabulous hybrid monster seats.

Maarten Baas
Hey Chair, Be A Bookshelf!
In his somewhat self-explanatory
Hey, Chair, Be A Bookshelf!
project, Maarten Baas changed
the function of otherwise
redundant items of furniture
and other random objects by
assembling them all into a giant
heap, reinforcing the pile with
polyester and handcoating
it with polyurethane. A chair
duly became a bookshelf, a
lampshade became a vase and a
violin, a coat rack. For the design,
Baas collaborated with several
secondhand stores in the region
of Eindhoven in the Netherlands,
taking products that could not
be sold in the shop. Since the
products are always different,
every piece is unique.

Will Gurley
Chair Back Stencils
Will Gurley's idea is to enable
anyone to make furniture
anywhere and everywhere. With
his Chair Back Stencil Kit and
the aid of a can of spray paint,
any wall, window, tree or other
vertical surface suddenly has
chair potential. Gurley created
four different chair backs for
the range: the Windsor Chair,
Charles Eames's Wire Mesh
Chair, and two Chippendale
designs. The stencil was created
for download, and can be printed
off in sections using a desktop
printer and then transferred onto
a larger piece of card stock.

-- Bamboo you --

Summer music festivals are great places to spot new resourceful ideas. When people who are used to a certain degree of civilization are suddenly forced to rough it for a weekend, all manner of invention and innovation spills forth. Caterers too, often require their furniture to be both robust and disposable – hence the bamboo table. A giant bamboo pole is wedged into the ground and a simple plywood disk with a hole in the centre slipped on top, supported by the ridges in the pole. It's surprisingly stable as well as being fast to put up, cheap and transportable.

-- A question of paste --

For a table that's seen too many coffee cups and wine glasses escape from the safe confines of their dedicated coasters, one idea is to use leftover wallpaper to revive it. It's a neater solution than a tablecloth and as simple as cutting the paper to fit and applying a layer of carpenter glue. Top the paper with a sheet of pre-cut glass or clear vinyl, or alternatively use vinyl-coated wallpaper in the first place to combat moisture and stains. It isn't a solution best suited to the mahogany family heirloom, granted, but if that's where your problem lies, let it be a lesson to take more care in the first place.

-- Rock formations --

If you want that old chair to really rock, the more accomplished woodworker should keep an eye out for scrap wood that can be affixed to the legs as rockers. Possible sources might be an old circular table top or a wooden sled.

-- Talking heads --

Some doors are too ornate and large to use as tabletops but they might well make good headboards for otherwise headboardless beds. Architectural salvage depots are the best places to find large doors, if you've not just moved into an old church or chateau, which may well come with a selection of its own to choose from.

Design example
WEmake
Rockit

London design group WEmake was established with the purpose of "laying bare and sharing the creative process". In other words, you make their products. Sort of. WEmake products – such as the Rockit instruction kit, which provides a template for cutting a pair of wooden rockers to add to a garden bench – have been designed to make users think about getting out their toolkits and making something.

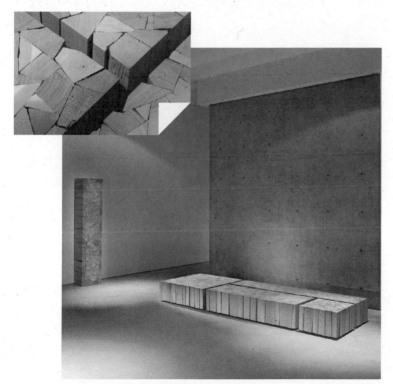

Design example
Brent Comber
Shattered

Using timber from fallen or already harvested trees, as well as cast-off materials from manufacturers and sawmills, Canadian designer Brent Comber creates furniture, artworks and installations that not only look incredible but also make little impact on the environment. Any leftover woodchips or sawdust are composted, completing a cycle of sustainability that returns nutrients to the soil.

Design example
Graypants
Scrap Furniture
Seattle-based Seth Grizzle and
Jonathan Junker trained as
architects, but set up Graypants
to allow them to get their hands
dirty designing and building
products and furniture. Some of
the duo's most popular products
are the Scrap ranges of chairs,
tables and light fixtures. "The
pure result of pillaging trash to
create elegant, useful products,"
the pieces are constructed
by layering plywood scraps,
cardboard or newspaper.

Scrapile

Bart Bettencourt and Carlos Salgado established Scrapile in New York in 2003. They have developed an efficient method for collecting and repurposing discarded scraps of wood from the city's woodworking industry. The ever-evolving line of furniture, produced under the banner of Scrapile, has a strong signature look that features striated bands of different coloured wood laminated together.

-- The great divide --

Screens and room dividers are all very well, but only if the room in question is big enough to screen or divide. If yours isn't, chances are the divider may work nicely as a headboard for your bed.

--Bean there done that --

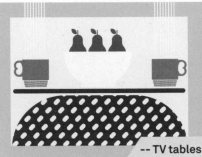

Top off a small beanbag with a smart circle of wood and turn it into a useful table for use on the side of the sofa or bed when you need to use a laptop or eat a meal. The solution works with larger beanbags to make footstools as well as canny alternative coffee tables.

-- TV tables --

If you are in the market for a feature table but can't splash out on a designer version, you can always afford to be inventive. Perhaps you have an old eight-track tape deck you want to keep but don't know what to do with, a huge retro television screen, or a strange artefact from a faraway land with a strong chassis. Whatever it is, there is usually a way it can be stabilized if need be, or mounted on some castors. A sheet of glass often makes the best top for the more unusual bases, as it won't spoil the view. Rubber cane tips or small pieces of cork may be necessary to protect the glass and prevent it from sliding.

-- Mirror image --

It is much more cost-effective to have an old mirror cut to spec (your local framer or glass-cutter will usually offer this service) and adhere it yourself to a shelf, table or cupboard door than it usually is to buy furniture ready-mirrored. On further reflection (pun intended) mirrors are often a brilliant way to revamp any old items of furniture that need resurfacing.

Nendo
Cabbage Chair

Constructed using waste paper from the pleated fabric industry, the Cabbage Chair was commissioned for the XXIst Century Man exhibition in Tokyo by fashion-house giant Issey Miyake. To make the deceptively simple chair, the Japanese design group Nendo wrapped the paper into a cylinder before slicing the resulting roll vertically halfway down on one side, and peeling back the layers to form the seat. Resins added during the paper production process give the form strength and durability, while the pleats also lend a bit of bounce. The chair is assembled without using any nails or screws.

STEP-BY-STEP

Pole position
- - - - - - - - - - - - - - - - -

It's not necessary to have billions in the bank or palatial surroundings to enjoy the decadence of waking up in a canopy bed every morning. It couldn't be easier to arrange. There are several variations on the theme but this may well be the easiest and most cost effective, because as long as you can hang a curtain rod, you can do this lying down, although you might want to save the lying-down bit until you're finished.

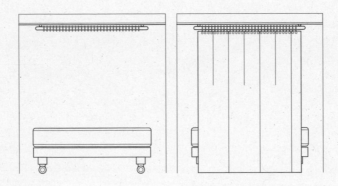

You will need:

_ A bed
_ Three curtain rods, lengths of broomstick, or thick dowel rod, the same length as the two sides and head of the bed.
– Six short lengths of plastic hose (2 cm long) if your curtain rods do not have built-in brackets.
_ Stud finder

_ Drill
_ Screws (about 5–7 cm long)
_ Screwdriver
_ Three curtains to fit the rods (old white sheets also work well). They should be long enough to reach the floor when suspended.
_ Curtain rings (not required if using tie-top curtains)

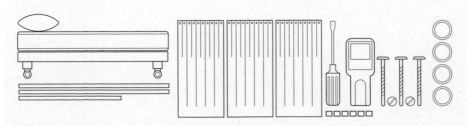

1_ Decide on the best position for the bed, taking into account the location of the ceiling beams (see 3).

2_ Run the curtain rings onto the rods (unless using tie-top curtains).

3a Use the stud-finder to locate the wooden ceiling beams. If you live in a building with metal beams (such as a modern block of flats) check a DIY guide for alternative instructions for hanging the curtain rods, and make sure you don't drill through any electric cables in the ceiling.

3b Position the rods so that they can be screwed into the ceiling beams, with one rod at the headboard of the bed, and the other two at the sides.

4a If using poles without brackets, drill through the curtain rods about 2 cm from each end.

4b Holding the rods against the ceiling in their final position, mark the location of the holes in the rods (or brackets), making sure you will be drilling into the ceiling beams, not just the plaster.

4c Drill into the marked points on the ceiling.

5_ If using rods without brackets, push the screws through the holes in the rods and through a piece of hose, which will act as a spacer between the rings and the ceiling.

6_ Screw the rods to the ceiling.

7_ Hang the curtains from the rings, put on your PJs and snuggle up in your new cocoon.

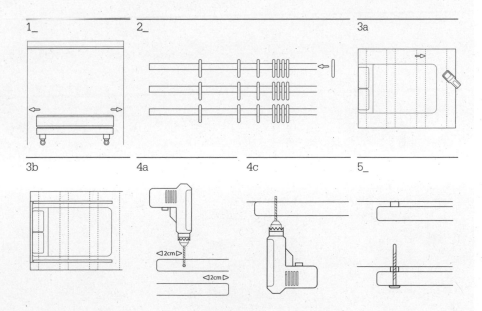

1_

2_

3a

3b

4a

4c

5_

Design example
Stanker Design
Motxo
Recycled oil barrels aren't something you might immediately associate with Parisian chic, but French designer François Royer began using them to make his line of side tables while based in the city in 2003. An artist with an ecological bent, Royer designs all his pieces – and they are all unique – based on a philosophy of recycling and using materials economically. Subsequently moving to the south of France, Royer followed up his recycled oil barrels with chairs made from abandoned supermarket shopping carts, a light-table made from a discarded washing-machine drum, and pencil holders made from painter's grids.

Design example
Jens Fager
RAW
Swedish designer Jens Fager shot to international acclaim when, fresh out of college, he produced a range of chairs, tables and candelabra as a bespoke project for chef Tommy Myllymäkio'o restaurant in Julita Gård, Sörmland. Originally called Grovhugget (Swedish for "rustic"), the items were created from pine using a band-saw, leaving rough-cut surfaces, which were then painted. The items were carved with the idea of emulating naïve cartoon sketches. The range later went into production for Swedish company MUUTO.

Amy Hunting
Patchwork Furniture
The Norwegian-born, London-based Amy Hunting is a designer and illustrator. Launched in 2008, her Patchwork Furniture is crafted from waste wood and offcuts collected from factories in Denmark. The wood fragments are glued together and carved to form new components for a chair, storage unit and series of twelve lamps. No screws or bolts are used in the making of the pieces, making them easily recyclable, should anyone ever actually want to.

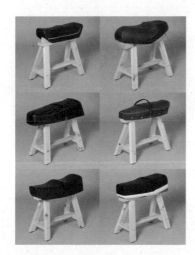

Design example

Emiliana Design
Vespa Cavallet
Ana Mir and Emili Padrós met in
1992 while studying industrial
design at Central Saint Martins
College of Art and Design in
London. The pair established
their studio, Emiliana, four years
later in Barcelona and went on
to carve out a serious reputation
for witty design. Vespa Cavallet
is an exercise in ad hoc furniture
– reusing the seat of a scooter.
Mir and Padrós designed several
versions of the stool, using
different makes and ages
of motorcycle – the base, in
pine, was made to fit each
individual seat.

-- Road tested --

The wheel was probably the most important invention of all time – without it we almost certainly wouldn't have tyre swings. First, find a tyre (truck tyres are best for adults, car tyres for littler people), a strong rope or chain and a good solid tree with a branch that can handle the weight of a person and a tyre without snapping. Positioning the swing near a pond, lake or river is a good idea if possible. Tie one end of the rope around one section of the tyre. Tie the other end of the rope around the tree branch. Make sure the knots can handle the weight as well as the rotation before going all-out monkey.

-- Fasten seat belts --

A novel and sturdy way to replace a worn-out seat cushion is to use a collection of leather belts. The straps should be woven together tightly across the top of the frame and buckled underneath. Use a utility or craft knife or an awl to cut extra holes in the belts if need be, and to trim off any excess leather.

-- Truck or treat --

While bicycle parts are common materials for the canny craftster, and redundant car parts can also be put to innovative good use, the innards of heavy goods vehicles are frequently overlooked. However, a redundant truck spring might well provide you with just the springy stool base you were looking for, and can be easily found if you know where to look – salvage warehouses and junkyards are a good starting place.

-- Case study --

Adapt an old hardshell suitcase into a lightweight, portable picnic or gaming chair with the addition of some serious stuffing inside each half of the open shell. Affix luggage straps at the sides, between the base and the lid, to keep the lid open at the right angle when seated, and when not in use simply pack the whole thing away.

Design example
Refunc.nl
Tyre Furniture
Preferring not to start from a design, Netherlands-based Refunc instead troubleshoots existing problems and improvises solutions using locally available waste materials. A car-tyre seating installation built in Durban, South Africa was their response to "the worst bus stops we ever saw." Sourcing 5000 brand new tyres that were unusable due to a production fault, they created a series of easy chairs. The firm's designers later built another tyre-seating installation at the architecture biennale in Venice, where they had to defend their raw materials from boatmen who wanted to use them as fenders.

STEP-BY-STEP

Peace and hammock

There's something infinitely romantic about a homemade hammock. It is so simple to construct and so comfortable to drift off in; it speaks of coconut palms and white sands even if it's just a place to nap in the garden shed. Adaptable, they can be stowed away when not in use, are easily washed and just as brilliant indoors as they are outside, especially positioned by a window with a view. Remember that people often fall out of hammocks, so use your common sense when positioning yours and test all knots before committing your full body weight.

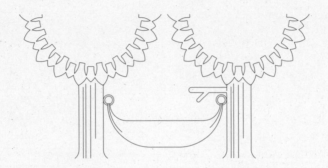

You will need:

_ A large sheet or any big piece of heavy-duty cloth such as canvas (about 3.5 m). If your hammock is going to be used outdoors, a waterproof fabric is preferable.

_ Six equal lengths of rock-climbing rope (or other rope that is designed specifically to hold the weight of a person). The length depends on how far apart the supports are, but you will need three for each side.

_ "O" ring anchor
_ Studfinder
_ Six eyehooks (5 cm)
_ Sewing machine and heavy thread
_ Trees or walls (ideally 3 to 5 m apart)
_ Two dowels (2 cm by 1.5 m)

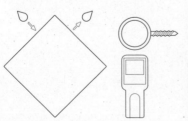

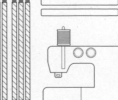

1_ Fold over 5 cm at each end of the canvas and stitch with a sewing machine and heavy-duty thread to create end flaps. Insert a dowel into each flap.

2_ Screw three eyehooks at even intervals onto each dowel.

3_ Thread each length of rope through an eyehook, securing in place with a bowline knot (see Step 6) or a round turn with two half hitches.

4_ Braid the lengths of rope at each end of the hammock.

5_ Fix the "0" ring anchor into a stud in the walls or tree from which you will hang the hammock.

6_ Tie the rope securely to the anchor or directly to the trees using a bowline or hammock-hanging knot.

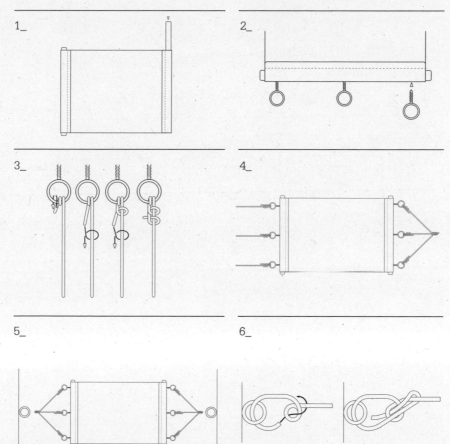

1_

2_

3_

4_

5_

6_

Design example
&made
Lost & Found
Lost & Found – a collection
by British design duo &made
– consists of disregarded
"found" furniture, regenerated
simply and quickly with a lick
of paint and reclaimed timber.

Ineke Hans
Fracture
Dutch designer Ineke Hans's
Fracture range takes inspiration
from broken limbs, and reinvents
the traditional plaster-cast
wrapping as a structural material
for furniture.

Design example
Frank Willems
Madam Rubens
Mattresses are one of the
most indigestible items for
waste-processing machinery,
forever getting jammed in the
shredders and generally causing
sleepless nights for facilities
managers. With the voluptuous
Madam Rubens collection Dutch
designer Frank Willems saves
redundant mattresses from the
shredder, strapping them onto
antique chairs before coating
the whole shebang in water-
resistant foam and then
painting it.

Design example
Anarchitect
Chairs
British architecture and design firm Anarchitect enjoyed success with its Seamless range of furniture in 2004. Rethinking the concept of upholstery, secondhand and found items of furniture were given a new lease of life with a seamless plastic coating. A quick dip in rubber not only updated the pieces, but also preserved their original forms and made them waterproof.

Design example
Studiomama
Pallet Furniture
Designer Nina Tolstrup was trained at Les Ateliers school of industrial design in Paris before going on to establish Studiomama in London. The pallet project was commissioned for a trade exhibition and was a huge success. Rather than churning out the items herself, however, Tolstrup opted to sell the instructions for making the range on her website. The pallet chair is made out of two pallets and 50 screws; the floor lamp requires just a single pallet, 15 screws, a bolt, some reused cable and a light fitting.

Design example
Raw Nerve
Life is Suite

Life is Suite is an upholstery system designed by Raw Nerve, which uses the client's keepsakes and ideas to create custom graphics and then applies them to an old favourite sofa. The idea came about when the Raw Nerve creatives found a battered and discarded sofa in the backstreets of Deptford. Taking it back to the studio, the group began to consider all the things that the sofa might have experienced in its long, evidently loved life. It could have been a child's castle or it might well have hosted two young lovers or even witnessed the tragedy of a failed marriage...things all got a little sentimental. Raw Nerve will often use secondhand tea cloths and aprons as upholstery.

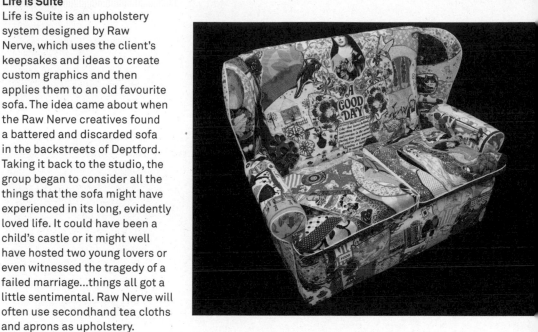

Design example
Majid Asif
Arm Chair

Credited with reviving the old art of papier mâché, Majid Asif's Arm Chair is made of 120 layers of newspaper built up over an inflatable mould. Each product is a unique creation whose surface appearance varies according to the paper used to create it, but the shape and size of each chair remains the same.

STEP-BY-STEP

Nice pad

With a little wave of your upholstery wand, that ugly duckling of a coffee table could turn into a beautiful swan of a cushioned ottoman. Depending on your raw materials, these instructions will also work to make an upholstered bench for a hallway or at the end of a bed.

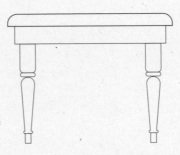

You will need:

_ An old table (make sure that your great grandmother wont be turning in her grave as you reinvent the family heirloom)
_ Sandpaper, primer and paint (optional for finishing)

_ Cotton batting
_ Foam (approximately 7 cm thick)
_ Electric or regular serrated knife
_ Spray adhesive
_ Scissors
_ Upholstery staple gun and staples
_ Flat head screwdriver for staple removal (just in case)
_ Upholstery fabric

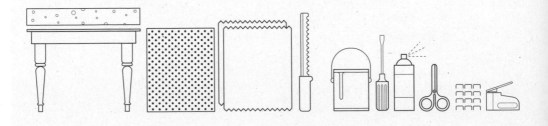

1_ Prepare the coffee table by finishing it as necessary. If it's in bad condition you may need to lightly sand, prime and paint it. This is also the best time to cut down the legs if you want to adjust the height.

2_ Lay out the foam on a flat work surface or the floor and place the coffee table upside down on top. Measure and mark the foam 2 cm around the edges of the table top, and mark up for cutting.

3_ Use the serrated knife to cut the foam (keep the knife blade at a right angle) along the marks.

4_ Spray one side of the foam with glue and position it on top of the table.

5_ Measure and cut a piece of cotton batting to cover the foam with an excess of 6 cm at each edge. Place it over the foam and staple in place. If you are covering a square or rectangular table start stapling at the centre of each side, and stop stapling 6 cm from each corner. This will enable you to finish corners in the same way as you would folding a flat sheet corner on a mattress – folded, tucked and pulled taut. Then you can staple them down securely.

6_ Lay your fabric over the top of the batting, and repeat the stapling process. Mark the fabric and cut off any excess when complete.

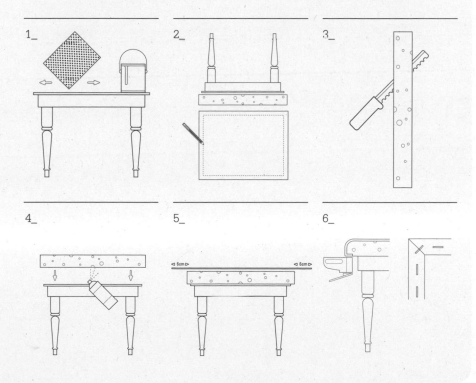

STORAGE

Boxes, drawers, files, hooks, jars, pots, rails
and shelves

-- Carton network --

While they might not be the most displayable (and they can always be decorated) milk, juice, soup and sauce cartons make handy pots for storing little things inside cupboards. Rinse the containers well and let dry; then fill them up with nuts and bolts, screws and nails, seeds, beads, ribbons or any other small items.

-- Carry on, nurse --

Fold up plastic supermarket bags and stuff them inside old medicine bottles where they can be kept discreetly around the house in places where they might one day be very useful, for instance, in the glove compartment of the car or under the kitchen sink.

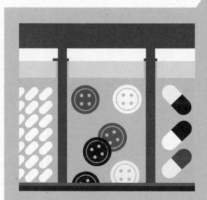

-- Tic Tactics --

Breath-mint boxes are perfect for storing and dispensing seeds, beads, sequins and pills – depending on your hobbies or requirements. As the boxes are cuboid and slim, they also pack neatly away into larger containers.

-- Fertile industry --

Obsolete and never again to be manufactured, an old floppy-disk container might be valuable one day, but it's quite unlikely. In the meantime, it is the perfect size for filing seed packets (alphabetically, or by season and plant-type), and waterproof to boot.

Design example

Boym Partners
Tin Man Canisters
Although not technically remaking as such, when Boym Partners convinced Alessi to reproduce the corrugated body of a standard tin coffee can for their Tin Man Canisters, it was in much the same spirit. Although more highly polished than the Boyms first intended, the end product became a design icon, emphasizing the structural strength and tactile gripping surface of a universal product, which the Boyms made no attempt to improve beyond the addition of a smart new lid. A spice-rack proposed for Droog Design in 1998 celebrated the classic shape of the humble jam-jar in similar fashion.

Design example
Jorre Van Ast
Jar Tops
Screw-on plastic additions to all standard sizes of glass jars, Jar Tops instantly transform the humble jam pot into all manner of more useful containers: sugar shaker, spice cellar, milk can, chocolate sprinkler, mug, water jug, oil-and-vinegar set – even a top to turn the jar into a generic storage container, making the seasoned remaker's kitchen look tidier and more coordinated.

-- Stocking fillers --

An old pair of tights makes a convenient sack for storing wrapping paper and posters to keep them from unrolling. Put a couple of rolls in each leg, then sling the tights over a coat hanger to and hang them up and out of the way.

-- A tissue? (bless you!) --

Keep the hard plastic boxes that baby-wipes are packaged in and use them to dispense tissues. This is an especially good idea in places where a cardboard tissue box would go soggy, such as in the bathroom or for camping.

-- Ice pack --

Oblong plastic ice-cream tubs are useful for storing all manner of things, from packed lunches to pet rocks. Ice-cream tubs also make good boxes for the first-aid kit kept in the bathroom or the car.

-- Feature comforts --

An ornate wooden headboard that you still like the look of but no longer want behind the bed can be adapted into a display shelf. Cut it in half horizontally to the desired height, attach brackets in a matching style, and paint to match your room.

-- Ticket tote --

A pouch on the fridge door for storing coupons, vouchers and receipts helps back pockets and handbags stay tidy. An old plastic CD case can be fashioned into just such a pouch. Tape the case open at a 30 degree angle and cover it with fabric or decorative paper before attaching a magnet or two to the back.

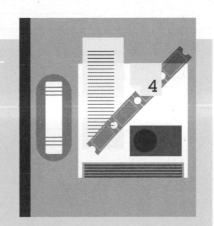

-- Brolly good --

Umbrella covers often get separated from their contents, or are left knocking around long after the umbrella itself has made its final exit. Reuse them to hold fabric shopping bags neatly and conveniently inside your handbag or briefcase.

-- Dispense with that idea --

An empty tissue box makes a useful dispenser for trash bags and other plastic bags that come in rolls. As well as stopping them from getting twisted up, the tissue box makes it easier to find the perforations as the bags are pulled out. Loose plastic bags can also be stored in the box so that they can be dispensed for reuse as needed.

-- Herbal medicine --

Who's got time to go to Scarborough Fair these days? For an indoor herb garden, transform empty milk cartons into planting containers by cutting the tops off with scissors or a kitchen knife, and punch a few holes in the bottom for drainage. Fill them with soil and sow with parsley, sage, rosemary and thyme.

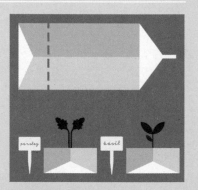

-- Poster girl --

Old whisky tubes make perfect storage containers for knitting needles, or, cut in half, for kitchen utensils. Knitting after a whole bottle of whisky can be dangerous, however. Please take care when implementing this tip.

Design example
Tim Brown
Idea* Cardboard Products
In an interesting commentary on how little people usually appreciate the value of packaging, Tim Brown's Idea* is a range of boxes that – while claiming to contain a product – actually don't. The product is the box itself, which can be deconstructed, turned inside-out and reconstructed as a piece of furniture.

New File
- - - - - - - - - - -

Procrastinating productively is an acquired skill. Some of the most time-tested traditions include snacking, filing and social networking. Why not combine all three by eating all the bran flakes, making the boxes into magazine files and giving them to your Facebook friends when you're finished.

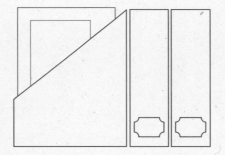

You will need:

_ Empty cereal box (large enough
   to hold your magazines or files)
_ Thicker cardboard for reinforcement
_ Scalpel or utility knife
_ Pen
_ Tape or glue
_ Labels and decorations (optional)

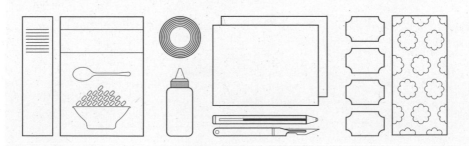

1_ Depending on the look you want for the final file, you can leave the cereal box as is, or disassemble it and reassemble with the brown side out for a cleaner aesthetic.

2_ Mark the reassembled box as shown to create two equal halves.

3_ Cut along the lines all around the box with the knife.

4_ If you plan to store heavy items such as magazines in the file it's a good idea to reinforce the box by gluing carefully cut pieces of thicker card to the insides, before decorating the outside to taste.

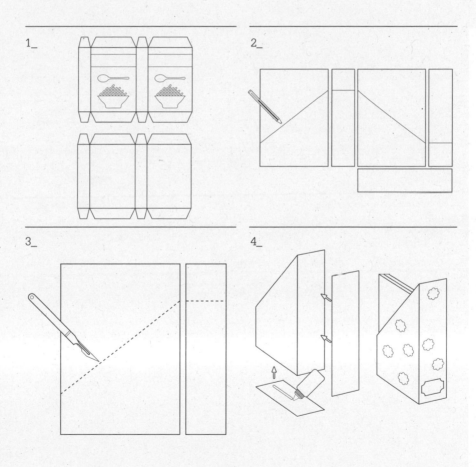

1_

2_

3_

4_

-- Popeye the saviour man --

Protein powder has muscled in on spinach as the bodybuilder's nourishment of choice these days. But what to do with those giant plastic jars it comes in? Fill one with sand, put a strap around the top and *voilà*: a handy kettlebell weight. Alternatively, if you live in an area prone to extreme weather, use the plastic canister to store a survival kit. For each person who might need rescuing, fill a canister with ready-to-eat nonperishable meals, including three breakfasts, three lunches and three dinners – just enough to help you all survive until your favorite superhero (or the emergency services) arrives with additional sustenance and aid. For more routine snacking emergencies, the containers also make good cookie jars.

-- Saucer inspiration --

Keep necklaces and other jewelry from getting tangled up in a box by organizing them in orphaned teacups and saucers arranged neatly in a drawer. It's a good idea to line the drawer first with a fabric such as felt or velvet to prevent the crockery from sliding around.

-- All of a clutter --

A well-stocked kitchen cupboard can house many delicious sauces, but an overcrowded one is a source of much frustration. Make it easier to retrieve that bottle of food colouring from the far back corner by keeping your pantry supplies organized on spare trays or baking tins inside the cupboard. As well as making it easy to slide the contents in and out as needed, it keeps the cupboard cleaner by catching drips and spills.

-- Divide and conquer --

To double up the space in a glassware cupboard, use an old tray as a shelf divider. First, line the tray with paper so that glasses stay put and won't be scratched. Arrange the glasses you use least often upside-down in the cupboard to form the lower supports. Place the tray over the glasses and stack smaller everyday glasses on top of it.

-- Sew right --

Refit an old glass Mason jar as a sewing kit by adding a neat pincushion on top. Trace around the rubber sealer on a piece of cardboard and use as a template to make a little pad the right size out of scrap fabric and stuffing. Glue the pad securely to the top of the lid. Keep your bobbins, scissors, needles and thimbles tidy inside the jar.

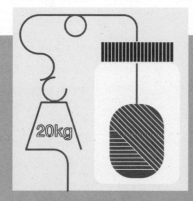

-- Sew strong --

If you're the sort of bodybuilder who is more into knitting than survival techniques (*see opposite*), plastic protein-powder containers make nice yarn holders. Use a drill to make a hole in the top and file the edges smooth so the yarn won't catch. Put the wool inside, feed the end through the hole in the lid, and knit away to your heart's content, safe in the knowledge that your yarn isn't going to get tangled.

-- Due notice --

Stretch large rubber bands over a flat tray, a piece of sturdy card or plywood to form an instant display board. You might also want to decorate the board first by painting it or covering it with paper. Add the bands, stretching them horizontally and vertically in a lattice, and slip your favourite pictures or stern to-do list behind them.

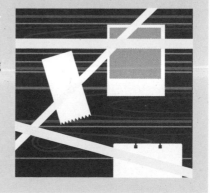

Design example
Studio Elmo Vermijs
Cratecupboard
Studio Elmo Vermijs, based in
the Netherlands, works across
the disciplines of architecture
and design, specializing in site-
specific projects that challenge
the use of space. Assembled
from a collection of secondhand
auction crates, shelves, beams
and offcuts, Cratecupboard is a
shelving system that can easily
be dismantled and moved when
necessary, or even used to store
other items while in transit.

-- Bracket sport --

For the seriously spatially challenged, many types of shelf brackets will double up nicely as hanging rails for clothes. Choose your bracket carefully (closed-loop ones are best) and position it where you want to hang your clothes. It's not a bad idea to put a shelf on top too, giving you a place to store folded T-shirts and sweaters.

-- Crate shakes --

Old wooden fruit crates make attractive storage boxes for just about anything. Attach four casters to the bottom of the box for mobility, and – depending on what you plan to store in the box – it might be worth lining it with extra wood (for strength), paper (for hygiene) or plastic (to catch any spillages).

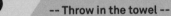

-- Throw in the towel --

Just because a ladder isn't safe for climbing anymore doesn't mean it won't make a brilliant towel rail in the bathroom. Paint it to look lovely and lean it over the radiator.

-- Ocean liner --

Cut up an old oilcloth table covering and use it to line storage boxes and baskets. The material is strong and water-resistant, so it's easy to clean and won't need hemming. Cut two strips the same width as the box, long enough so that when you lay them crosswise inside the box, they cover the bottom and sides with a few inches to spare at each edge. Fold the excess oilcloth over the edge of the box, and use a punch to make holes at each corner of the overhang. Tie the corners together with string or ribbon threaded through the holes.

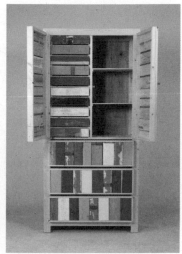

Design example
**Piet Hein Eek
Scrapwood Cupboards**
Dutch furniture designer
Piet Hein Eek's Scrapwood
Cupboards, which he began
making in 1990 from bits of
found wood and salvaged
materials, became his
trademark. Celebrating the
textures of the materials rather
than trying to disguise them, the
designs provided a refreshing
alternative to mass-produced
furniture. The range expanded
over the years to include
patchwork one-of-a-kind chests,
dining tables, chairs and sofas.

Design example

**Checkland Kindleysides
1 Fournier Street**
Interior design company
Checkland Kindleysides was
commissioned by the Timberland
Boot Company to create a new
type of "trading space" in an old
banana warehouse. With the aim
of building as little as possible,
the designers repurposed the
fittings that were already there:
box rolling-racks unearthed from
the basement became display
tables and cardboard banana
boxes were stacked to create
a stockholding wall at the rear
of the store.

Design example
MCDBLJ
Crates
Belgrade designers MCDBLJ
repurposed a series of old
fruit crates as storage for
an exhibition in 2007 called
Redesign Your Mind, which
also featured cupboards
made from vintage wooden
voting boxes.

Design example
M:OME
Doublewood Shelf
American architects Laura
Joines-Novotny and Tom di
Santo, established a product arm
of their practice M:OME called
MOMElife in 2002. Striving for
what they describe as greater
"eco-literacy" the pair's mission
is to "create modern design
that re-thinks its purpose". The
Doublewood shelf is a product
that uses up the odd-shaped
leftover pieces of hardwood
that normally get thrown out.

-- Vindaloo sunset --

No need to throw a Tupperware party to save on plastic food-storage containers – simply eat more takeaways and save the packaging. Glass jars also make good containers for leftover foods and are probably safer for heating food in the microwave than the plastic packing supplied.

-- Cellophane noodles --

It can pain domesticated environmentalists to throw away the pretty cellophane that sometimes comes wrapped around flowers from the florist. Instead, many a paragon of old-fashioned frilly-apron-wearing homeliness has been known to reuse it to make little bags for cookies, candies and cakes at holiday time – just be sure to wash it well if using it for food.

-- Brown paper packages --

Lovely crisp paper bags from market stalls can be kept and used to ripen fruit – especially useful for avocados or tomatoes. Keep them in a dark spot for three or four days and maybe put a lime or a ripe apple in with them to speed up the process – both are an excellent source of the ripening agent ethylene.

-- Hanging bulbs --

Tights can be very useful for storing fresh garlic – just drop in a bulb, knot the tight, and repeat until the leg is full – whereby it can hang up in the pantry (or wherever) until it's needed. Stored like this the garlic stays usable for much longer than if it's been left loose on the shelf or abandoned somewhere in the back of the fridge.

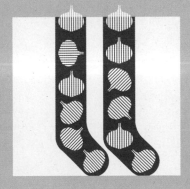

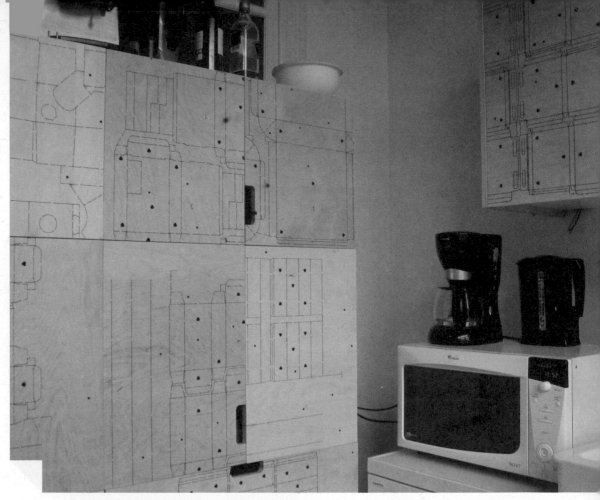

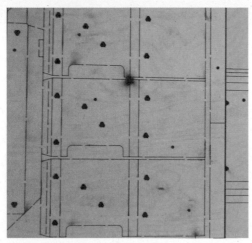

Design example

Rotor
Kitchen Units

Brussels-based Rotor specializes in reusing industrial waste in architecture and design projects. The panelling of these kitchen cupboards is made from laser-cut plywood, formerly used as punching-plates, from a company that die-cuts cardboard for luxury-goods packing.

Cabinet reshuffle

If you can come by an old kitchen cupboard unit – perhaps in your local junkyard, or perhaps if you have just had your own kitchen refitted – it can be nicely repurposed as a number of useful furniture items, from a toy box to a plush ottoman.

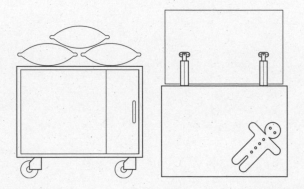

You will need:

_ Kitchen cupboard unit
_ Plywood
_ Safety hinges
_ Drawer paper (if lining)

_ Paint (optional, for finishing)
_ Sandpaper (optional, for finishing)
_ Pillows or fabric and foam to make a homemade cushion (for Step 3b)
_ Castors (for Step 3c, optional)
_ Finials (for Step 4, optional)

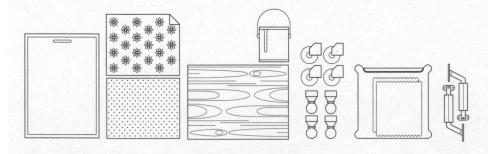

1_ Depending on the condition of the cabinet to begin with, you may want to line it with drawer paper and/or give it a lick of paint.

2_ For a child's desk, position the cabinet upright against a wall. Cut a work surface from a piece of plywood so that it is just larger than the top of the cabinet, and fix it with hinges at the top rear edge of the cupboard so that it can be flipped up and leaned against the wall when not in use.

3a For a new ottoman or storage bench (an ideal place to keep games, DVDs and old magazines) turn the cabinet on its side and refinish the surface as necessary.

3b Top the item off with a couple of pillows or, for a more polished look make a bespoke pad [see pp. 52–53 for detailed instructions].

3c Add castors to the bottom so that you can move the ottoman around easily.

4_ Turn the same old cabinet onto its back and you have an instant toy chest. Add safety hinges to the cupboard door to make a secure and child-friendly lid. Salvaged wooden finials or spindles from staircase-railings can optionally be attached to the underside of the chest for feet.

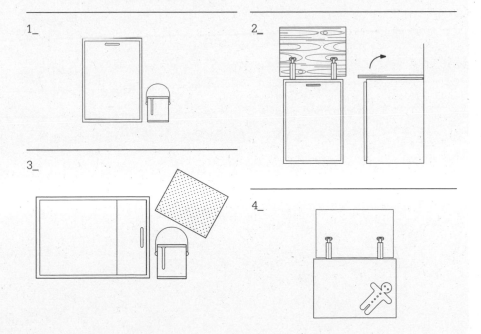

1_

2_

3_

4_

-- Room with a view --

Windows are for looking into as well as looking out of. An attractive window that is no longer required as a porthole to the world can be repurposed as the door of a cabinet or the front of a shelving unit, attached using a set of sturdy hinges.

-- Disk world --

The designer of the humble CD spindle probably never knew that one day it might also make an ingenious toilet-paper dispenser. A couple of neat cuts might sometimes be necessary (depending on the design of the spindle) and it can also be decorated by lining the clear plastic lid with attractive paper. Otherwise, fix the spindle to the toilet lid or bathroom wall for a cat- and puppy-proof solution.

-- Tower of bagel --

Sometimes the universe presents us with combinations so brilliant and so unexpected that it is nothing short of awe-inspiring. When Flickr user Rodrigo Piwonka discovered he could use an old CD spindle as an instant lunchbox for a bagel, he knew he had found a match made in heaven and posted it on the website. The idea travelled around the world in a matter of minutes, and Piwonka's name is now synonymous with "bagel box" on Google.

-- Willing and cable --

CD spindle cases – when they are not containing bagels or toilet paper – make very convenient cable tidies. For a tangle-free desk, simply coil up the power and computer cables loosely inside the see-through case. This method can also be used to keep headphones tidy and accessible.

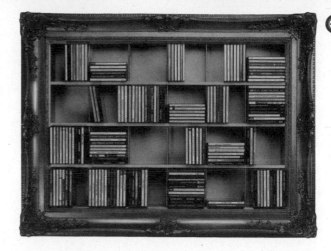

Design example
**Franz Maurer
Vienna**
For those who like to have their music collections on display, the Vienna makes a point of it. The statement shelving solution by Viennese designer Franz Maurer (for German manufacturer Anthologie Quartett) uses an antique lacquered wood frame as a wall-mounted display case.

Design example
**Jo Meesters and
Marije van der Park**
Believing there could be more to a makeover than a lick of paint and a piece of plywood, in 2005 Meesters began a series of projects in collaboration with Marije van der Park to improve and revitalize discarded items of furniture using new techniques. Two experiments involved sandblasting and perforating the wood, as seen on this cupboard.

Design example
Jens Praet
One Day Paper Waste
The One Day Paper Waste
collection by Belgian designer
Jens Praet is constructed
from shredded confidential
documents. Mixed with resin the
paper is then compressed into a
mould to form different items of
furniture. Initially designed for an
exhibition in 2007 in Eindhoven
(in the Netherlands), the line was
quickly put into production by
Droog Design. A bespoke storage
unit in black resin was later
commissioned by L'Uomo Vogue,
in a collaboration with Italian
underwear brand Yamamay.

Design example
Adrien Rovero
Barrel
Adrien Rovero's Barrel series
of low-level tables and storage
units is made using traditional
barrel construction techniques,
giving rustic, time-honoured
designs a contemporary twist.
The Swiss-based designer
constructed the limited-edition
pieces exclusively for Gallery
Libby Sellers in 2008.

-- Tray chic --

The polystyrene or plastic fruit trays that supermarket fruit sometimes comes in can be reused to tidy up a chaotic drawer. Keep socks neatly in pairs, or use them as organizers for keys, paper clips and small random items.

-- Bristle a new tune --

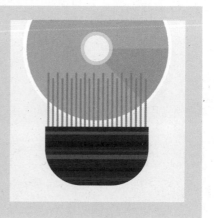

A broom head, thoroughly washed and still in good condition, can be put to use as a novel storage system for all sorts of items, including CDs, letters and photos. For a table-top version, mount an old hairbrush on a piece of scrap wood or other suitable base to make a slightly ridiculous desk-tidy, or a hair-accessory holder for your dressing table.

-- Clipped accent --

Glue a strip of strong magnet to the back of a clothes peg or bulldog clip and stick it to the fridge for a handy way to hang tea towels in the kitchen. The magnetized clips can also be used to hold oven mitts, friendly notes to housemates, comedy aprons, sensible money-off coupons, glamorous party invitations, hilarious photographs, interesting newspaper clippings, tasty recipes, wishful shopping lists or even crayon drawings of dinosaurs. Anything goes.

-- Clothes line --

Two secret wardrobe storage staples that every sartorialist worth her dry-cleaning bill will know: newspaper and plastic bags. Rolled-up newspapers can be used as boot trees to stop damp boots from loosing their shape; stored garments stay crease-free when individually wrapped in a plastic bag. Handbags that don't see a lot of use should also be stuffed with newspaper or inflated plastic bags before storing in order to prevent deflation.

Design example
Tejo Remy
Chest of Drawers
In his first exhibition for Dutch
design collective Droog,
Tejo Remy assembled an
eclectic collection of recycled
drawers randomly arranged
and balanced as a new storage
unit. The drawers are encased
in individual purpose-made
maplewood boxes, which
are then bound together
with a jute strap.

STEP-BY-STEP

Kitchen leftovers

It's entirely possible to build a complete fitted kitchen from scrap timber
and secondhand furniture. If you can't find everything you need in the street
on trash collection day, salvage yards usually offer fabulous components,
from sinks to sideboards, for very good prices.

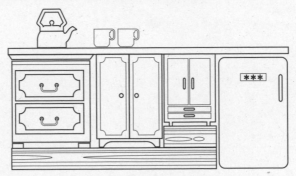

You will need:

_ Your choice of salvaged storage
furniture (items of a similar period,
in the same wood or colour is ideal)
_ Your choice of kitchen appliances
(e.g. cooker, stove top, dishwasher,
washing machine, freezer, fridge)

_ Saw
_ Sandpaper
_ Hammer and nails
_ Screwdriver and screws
_ Handles and hinges
_ Paint or woodstain (optional)
_ Worktop
_ Spare wood for kickboards (optional)

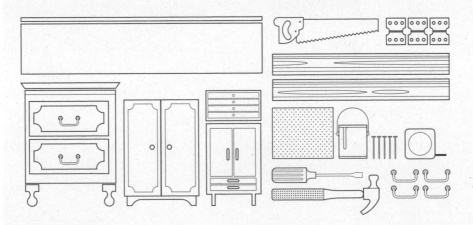

1_ Carefully measure your kitchen and draw out your design in detail. It might even be worth constructing a scale model to ensure the arrangement will fit the available space and accommodate all of your appliances.

2_ Fix and refurbish any items that need a bit of TLC, replacing any worn-out hinges and handles at this stage. Matching handles will visually unify a random collection of salvaged units.

3_ Once you have assembled and repaired all the components, the hard part is getting them all to the same level. Standard worktop height is 90 cm, so some pieces may need to be cut down, while others can be raised on a subframe.

4_ If you are adding wallmounted units, remember that in a standard kitchen these should be around half the height of the countertop – i.e., approximately 45 cm if using a standard 90 cm worktop height.

5_ Add a kickboard in places where you have had to raise the furniture. Kickboards should sit about 5 cm back from the fronts of the units. For an optional finishing touch, consider painting or staining all the units and kickboards the same colour.

6_ Level off the units with a new work surface – this horizontal element is likely to be the dominant feature of the kitchen and adds uniformity to your otherwise charming vintage hotchpotch, so its inclusion is very important. It's the one component that is really worth getting from a kitchen specialist to make sure it fits well, although if you fancy yourself a pro joiner you certainly could save yourself a fair bit of money.

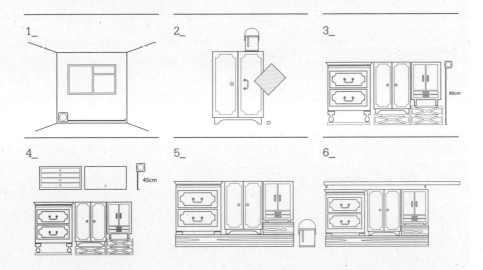

1_

2_

3_   90cm

4_   45cm

5_

6_

-- Soap opera --

Even outside the bathroom, a wall-mounted soap dish can make a useful little shelf just inside the front door for loose change or keys, or even an elegant paperclip tray on the wall beside the desk. A spare soap dish can also be used to hold matches beside the fireplace, jewelry on a dressing table, or as an ashtray behind the bike shed.

-- Fly liner 1 --

Use up that single roll of vintage wallpaper or sheet music by lining the back walls of a cupboard or shelving unit. Not only will it be a nice surprise every time you open the cupboard doors, but you won't have to worry so much about matching it to the rest of the room.

-- Fly liner 2 --

Sturdy, hard wearing and (often) pretty, leftover wallpaper can also be used to line your dresser drawers. Measure the inside of the drawer first and cut the paper with a pair of scissors. Fix it in place with a little glue or blue tac in each corner if needed.

-- Trees lounge --

Get back to nature and fashion a mug tree, or indeed a ring tree, from a real tree. Choose a few interesting branches with horizontal offshoots, plant them in a vase filled with rocks or sand, and hang your chosen objects from the shoots.

-- Knife and easy --

If you are an artist and have a piece of vinyl drawing-board covering going spare, or if you know an artist who might let you take it off their hands, try using scraps of it to line kitchen drawers. The material is ideal for storing implements such as knives, as its rubbery texture stops them from sliding around, and is also easy to clean.

Michael Marriott
Four Drawers

When he designed this drawer unit in 1996, Michael Marriott was not – as he was later pigeonholed – pioneering recyling in design. Instead the London based practitioner found qualities in certain products that were not being utilized in their current incarnations, and decided to draw attention to the fact. The drawers are constructed from birch plywood, pegboard and Spanish fruit crates.

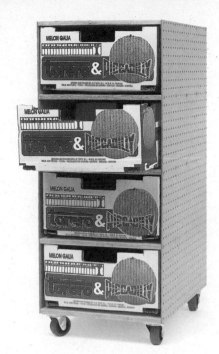

Kako.ko
Totem

Serbian design studio Kako.ko looked at some Styrofoam packaging and saw a bookshelf. Emphasizing the aesthetic value and longevity of Styrofoam by giving the packaging a new function, the designers also wanted to draw attention to the fact that the material is rarely recycled, which is why its deployment in single-use food- and drink-packaging is banned in many countries.

Design example
JAM
Robostacker
JAM is a design and
communications agency that
works with companies to give
their products fresh spin. In a
project for Whirlpool, intended to
reach a new base of design- and
lifestyle-conscious consumers,
JAM initiated a recycling project
in which four pieces of furniture
were constructed from washing
machine drums: the Drum Stool,
the Drum Table, the Robostacker
(storage), and the Hoola-Hoop
(display), which were sold and
exhibited in museums, galleries
and design shops.

-- Tread carefully --

Ladders and stepladders that don't see a lot of action can be a pain to store in small homes. Keep yours in service by converting it into shelving with the addition of a few boards over the treads. A stepladder may already have treads large and sturdy enough to hold a few paperbacks without needing further modifications.

-- Veg out --

Retain the deep vegetable drawers from a retired refrigerator and use them to store root vegetables such as potatoes and onions in a dark cupboard.

-- Draw up a plan --

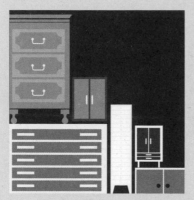

During the Edo period in Japan there was a popular storage system called the *kaidan-dansu* ("step-chest") consisting of drawer units stacked up to allow them to double as a staircase. Taxes were higher for two-storey houses, so when the collectors came to call, the *kaidan-dansu* that usually led up to the second level would simply be moved to another part of the room in the hope that the extra space would not be noticed.

-- Cool customer --

The shelves and trays from an otherwise unwanted refrigerator can have a useful new life in the bathroom, where their wipe-clean and waterproof qualities really come into their own. All egg racks are different, but some shapes (those with holes rather than moulded recesses) provide the perfect sink-tidy for toothpaste and toothbrushes.

-- Separate lives --

Your local grocery store will often be happy to offload cardboard boxes should you need them for moving. Particularly useful are the sort that have been used to transport bottles, as they come with removable dividers that are perfect for keep cleaning products organized under the kitchen sink.

-- Nice rack --

Use an old wooden plate-rack to keep saucepan lids tidy in a cupboard. The same solution also works well for expanding collections of Tupperware, while for those who have lots of unruly small containers in a drawer, a toast rack might suffice.

-- Scrap heap --

Cut off the top of an empty milk or fruit-juice carton and keep it to hand as a countertop bin to store scraps while you're cooking. If you're separating your food waste, keep three cartons on the counter for easy sorting: vegetable peelings for stock, compostables for the compost heap, and fats, cooked food and animal products for the rubbish.

-- Blade runners --

If you're a fair-weather gardener and your secateurs only snip into action in springtime, it's important to store them (and other gardening tools) somewhere where they won't get rusty. Fill an old bucket or coffee can with sand mixed with a litre or so of (clean) motor oil. Plunge the metal parts of trowels, forks and shears into the sand mixture to keep them lubricated, rust-free and tidy.

-- Moth broth --

If you hate the smell of mothballs, you don't have to risk holey sweaters for lack of moth ammunition when storing your woollens. Pencil shavings (which are typically made of cedar wood) work just as well. Collect the shavings after sharpening sessions and tie them in little cloth bags before storing them with your clothes in wardrobes and drawers. The moths, thus repelled, will have to do their munching somewhere else.

-- A case for hanging --
A wooden clothes-horse can be put back into service as a rack for magazines and newspapers. Sheets of wrapping paper and scrap fabrics can be displayed in the same way, ready to hand should one suddenly have the urge to wrap something up.

-- Exhibit A --
A ready-made wall-mounted plate rack is wasted on crockery. In the nursery it will make a great compartmentalized shelf for displaying children's books and small toys, while it can also be a useful organizer in the home office.

-- (There must be) 50 ways to leave your louvre --
Wooden shutters used indoors will make an attractive and useful display board. Just mount one on a wall and tuck invitations, artworks and messages into the louvres. Remember, if the shutters you are using feature adjustable louvres, you'll need lock them in position first; otherwise everything will fall out, which rather defeats the point.

-- Welly good idea --

If you need an umbrella stand (and who doesn't?) the most traditional solution is the spare Wellington boot. Decorate the outside if you like, line the inside with a plastic bag, and fill the bottom of the boot with sand or pebbles to make sure it stays upright when it's filled with soggy brollies.

Design example

**Michael Cross and Julie Mathias
Lunuganga**
Michael Cross and Julie Mathias
approach design by "taking an
object we know and beginning
again". In 2004 the pair spent two
weeks in the late Geoffrey Bawa's
fairytale retreat Lunuganga in Sri
Lanka, which inspired this design
for a shelving unit that brings a
little bit of jungle into the living
room. (The branch was cast in
polyurethane, but the remaking
spirit is evident.)

STEP-BY-STEP

Closed brackets

The invisible bookshelf has become such a classic novelty item that it's unlikely to baffle people as much as it once did. However it's still a very useful way to make a small, quirky shelf, and to reuse an old book while you're at it. *Harry Potter* works well for this repurpose – it has all the right magical qualities as well as being ginormous.

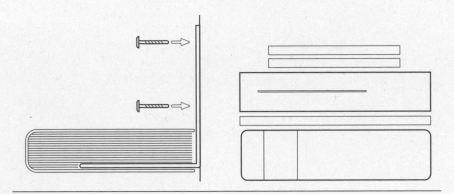

You will need:

_ A book that you never intend to read again but don't mind being permanently displayed on your wall. Classics are good – first editions probably not.
_ L-shaped shelf bracket
_ Scalpel or utility knife
_ Pen
_ Screwdriver
_ Screws
_ Tape measure
_ Superstrong glue
_ Something heavy to use as a weight

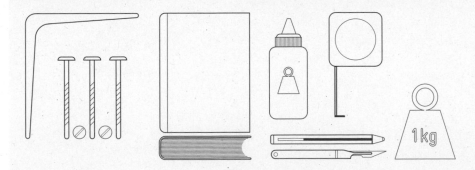

1_ Use the tape measure to find the centre of the book. Mark the point on the inside back page.

2_ Position your bracket so that it is aligned with the centre mark. In the finished shelf the bracket will hold the weight of the book with its spine facing outward. Draw an outline around the bracket.

3_ Trace around the bracket outline with the knife, cutting a hole in the pages so that the bracket will set flush.

4_ Use your knife to make a notch in the cover deep enough for the vertical section of the bracket. This is to allow the book to sit flush against the wall.

5_ Secure the bracket in place with screws.

6_ It's worth putting a screw through the pages towards the edges of the book to keep them together. Put some pressure on the pages while doing this to keep them in line.

7_ Glue the bottom cover of the book into place. Weight heavily, and wait overnight.

8_ Screw it all to the wall and stack up books on top to hide the bit of the bracket you can see. Magic.

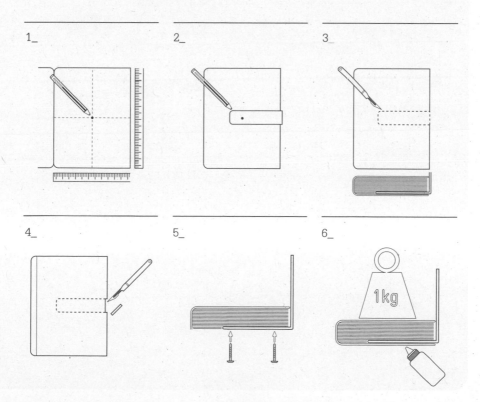

1_

2_

3_

4_

5_

6_

LIGHTING &
ACCESSORIES

Lamps and lampshades, crockery and

cutlery, vases, bookends and candlesticks

-- Drain on resources --

A clean terracotta pot set atop a saucer makes simple but effective cutlery drainer. You could decorate it with a lick of waterproof paint or glue-on decorations, if you wanted to.

-- What's hooking? --

There is no end to the objects that will happily repurpose themselves as pegs for hanging coats and keys. From rustic finds such as sticks and stones, to architectural salvage items like old taps and doorknobs, or kitsch objects like toys and video game joysticks, if you can fix it to a wall so that it sticks out in a manner that allows you to hang things off it, you might as well call it a hook.

-- To the wire --

Stretch a piece of chicken wire across the back of an oversized wooden picture frame to form a memo board. Use wire cutters to cut the wire to fit and spray-paint it black (or any other colour) before fixing it to the frame using a staple gun (please wear gloves). Use little hooks and bulldog clips to attach photos and notes to the board.

-- Hang it all --

All those wire hangers accumulated from drycleaners can be prettied up with simple cardboard slipcovers. Jackets and shirts will hang better and last longer, while the addition of small pegs or hooks to the lower part of the hanger will also hold skirts and dresses very effectively. Create a template before you cut the cardboard so that all the hangers are uniform. Another way to revamp them is to match them up in pairs, and wrap them in wool or string to make thick and colourful (if you like) bespoke clotheshangers.

Brave Space Design
Mountain Range Coatrack
The designers at Brave Space Design in Brooklyn, New York, love bamboo and have created all sorts of furniture items from the super-sustainable material, including shelving units shaped like Tetris blocks, and attractive dining tables and chairs. The group also frequently uses scrapwood in its work. One example is the Mountain Range Coat Rack, which takes advantage of the graded colours found through an offcut plank of wood that the designers have cut away to create snowy white mountain peaks off which to hang one's coat.

Alex Hellum
Thoughts on Furniture
In 2001 designer Alex Hellum held his first solo show in Stavern, Norway, entitled Thoughts on Furniture. In it he explored how people use furniture beyond the intentions of the designer, a theme that has consistently informed his work ever since. Usually his pieces involve building in an unexpected use for an ordinary product, for example, his peg chair – a bedroom chair that incorporates a coat-stand. Other projects find unexpected uses for defunct pieces of furniture. Perhaps the best example of the latter is the series of wall-mounted coat hooks, lovingly made in his workshop in a bid to salvage the beautifully turned legs of otherwise unusable chairs.

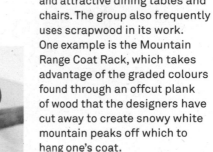

Design example
Marina Bautier
Keyplug
Designed by Belgian designer Marina Bautier for her own company, La Maison de Marina, the wall-mounted Keyplug is perfect for households where keys are always getting mislaid. And if the keys aren't plugged in where they should be, it's a pretty safe bet where else they might end up. Flatmates should be warned of the possible dangers of this one.

Junktion
Soccer Players Hanger
Founded in 2008 by a group
of designers based in Tel
Aviv, Junktion aims to rethink
everyday objects and use them
in new contexts. When their
reserve fusbol players aren't on
the pitch, they make themselves
useful taking people's coats.

Design example
Junktion
Backrest Hanger
One of the collective's first
projects involved cutting a
child's chair in half and affixing
the two halves to a wall to create
both a useful hanging space for
coats and a shallow shelf that
makes an ideal home for keys.

-- Utter display --

An innovative alternative to framing photographs, posters, or other pictures is to clamp them into an old wooden skirt or trousers hanger. Those with a single strip-clamp – some are even lined with felt – will work best, as clips might damage the image, but all sorts of different types will do the job nicely.

-- Network rail --

Just as plumbing parts can be reassembled to create candlesticks, so can the more ambitious hoarder of pipes construct a bathroom hanging rail. Assemble the pipes and fittings in the most convenient arrangement to suit your household and *voilà* – all that's left to do at the end of this satisfyingly straightforward DIY exercise is to throw in the towel.

-- Bright ideas --

Any unwanted large glass vessel can be turned into a lamp just by filling it with Christmas lights. Even an old wine bottle can be made to look pretty this way – remove the labels first, and secure any trailing cord to the back of the bottle using a thin strip of clear adhesive tape.

-- Wax much? --

Melt down old candle stubs in a double boiler (or a glass bowl placed in a saucepan of boiling water) to make new ones. Glass jam jars can make good receptacles, as can old tin cans, pots or lone drinking glasses that have lost their set. Wick can be bought from any craft store, but you can also make your own by braiding three pieces of 100% cotton string. Pour the wax around the wick, holding the string in place while it cools by placing a pencil across the top of the jar and laying the end of the wick over it.

Design example
Rita Botelho
Lighting Ball
For this range of side lamps
by Portuguese designer
Rita Botelho, Christmas lights
are coiled up inside the little
plastic balls from automatic
gift-vending machines. The
idea, she says, is to "bring alive
a playful symbolic universe,
using objects well known from
our childhood". The plastic balls
have two halves, one transparent
and the other coloured, giving
different lighting effects, and
as both the balls and the
Christmas lights can be found
in different shades, a wide
variety of colour combinations is
possible. The lights are specially
prepared so that they can come
in direct contact with plastic
without overheating.

Design example
Sergio Silva
Oyule Lamp
As amateur ecologists
everywhere begin to see the light
and replace their incandescent
bulbs with more sustainable
alternatives, the traditional
glass-and-filament lightbulbs
are to become relegated to
history. US-based Portuguese
designer Sergio Silva has
transported the product back in
time and repurposed it as an oil
lamp, substituting a wick where
the filament once was.

STEP-BY-STEP

Ping-Pong Merrily on High

Revive and upgrade a string of Christmas lights by making little covers for the bulbs. Ping-pong balls are perfect ready-made shades as they diffuse the light attractively and are cheap and easy to come by.

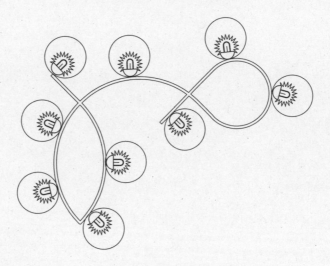

You will need:

- String of Christmas lights
- A ping-pong ball for each light on the string
- Drill and drill bit
- C-clamp
- Hot glue
- Glue gun

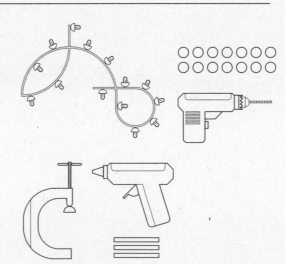

1_ Before you start, check the ping-pong balls for dents, especially if you are using old balls. Place any that are less than perfect in a pan of boiling water for a few minutes to restore them to their former spherical glory.

2_ Check the lights for any electrical shorts or overheating bulbs before starting.

3_ Holding the ping-pong ball steady in the clamp, drill a hole in it using a drill bit slightly thinner than the bulbs.

It is a good idea to test-fit the first ball over a bulb before drilling the rest.

4_ When you have punctured enough balls, slide one over each bulb.

5_ To stop the balls from being knocked off, apply a little hot glue around where the base of the light fixture meets the ping-pong ball. (This step might not be necessary if the fit is good enough originally.)

6_ String up the lights and bask in the glow of another job well done.

1_

2_

3_

4_

5_

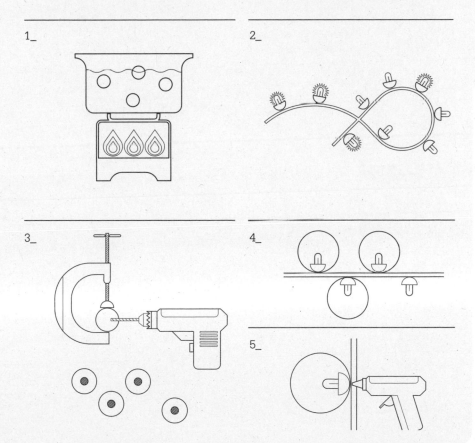

Design example
Amplifier
Champagne Cork Coathook
A memorable bottle of champagne can forever be preserved on the wall as a coathook. Florian Kremb, founder of Amplifier, began making them to order when he noticed how champagne corks are not only the perfect shape for hanging a coat or jacket, but that they can also provide a memento of a good party, wedding or other celebration.

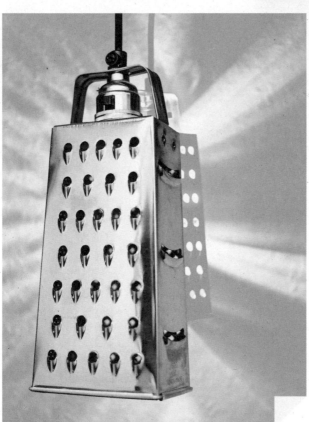

Design example
Amplifier
Cheesegrater Light
"Cheese electric – she's got a family full of eccentrics." Perhaps the lyrics to the famous Oasis song were inspired by this cheesegrater lampshade. Similar to the colander lamp, this object designed by Amplifier takes a fresh look at the form of everyday kitchen utensils. Leaving its common purpose aside, each side of the grater projects a different and intriguing light show into the room. The handle provides a convenient holder for the light fitting.

-- Finial countdown --

Should you have recently dismantled the banisters of an old staircase, balustrade finials or long spindles can be put to new use as candlesticks. Drill a hole for a tall candle or balance a tealight on top, placing a metal disk (available from craft shops) underneath the burning candle. Add a base if necessary to ensure that the end result is stable. Fire away.

-- Cork in the act --

The two most common uses for cork in the home are corkboards and wine stoppers. Use the latter to make a new version of the former by collecting up a few, slicing them in half lengthways and mounting them onto a board round side-up. The ideal backing might be an old picture frame that has lost its glass but otherwise any piece of board will do, and a tidy edge can be made from square wood on dowels or with a strip of ribbon. Use heavy-duty glue to fix the flat sides of the corks down to the backboard.

-- Wined and dined --

Old corks – whether real or plastic – make perfect stands for hot pans. Arrange the corks tightly inside an adjustable metal pipe clamp and use a screwdriver to tighten the clamp around them; then stage a dinner party to show off your new trivet. Corks can also be sliced and fixed together for coasters. Although variation in the colour of the corks can be pretty, its possible to remove red-wine stains from the corks by soaking them in bleach and water solution (4 tablespoons of bleach for every cup of water). Rinse and allow to dry before using.

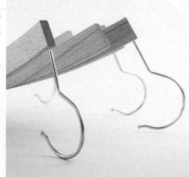

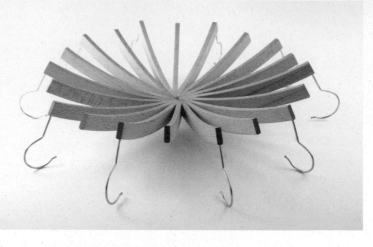

Design example
Amplifier
Coat Hanger Fruit Bowl
Florian Kremb of Amplifier has
fashioned a fruit bowl from a
number of conventional crescent
coat hangers.

Design example
Dominic Wilcox
War Bowl
In the heat of the battle – or
perhaps the microwave – all the
little plastic soldiers melted. The
end result was a novelty fruit
bowl. One of designer Dominic
Wilcox's best-selling products,
the War Bowl uses both French
infantry and British artillery from
the Battle of Waterloo set. Other
versions include knights and
black-and-red ninjas.

**Loyal Loot
Log Bowls**
Doha Chebib's collection uses wood felled by storms, or cut down due to re-landscaping and development. Chebib works with local craftspeople to gather the wood, and turn the sections by hand on a lathe, finally painting and sealing the inside of the bowl to a bright glossy finish. Canadian-based Chebib is part of a collective called Loyal Loot devoted to working with natural materials that age well.

-- **Key note** --
A defunct typewriter or computer keyboard can be happily
reincarnated as fridge magnets, as can old sets of Scrabble
letters and other board-game counters. With strong enough
magnets, or stickyback mounting, chess pieces – in particular
the pawns – can make interesting hooks for small items.

-- **Easy as ABC** --

It isn't often that a person can claim to have a better
vocabulary the more beer they drink. To make it true, save
the bottle tops to make your own alphabet fridge magnets.
Glue or wedge a magnet into the recess and apply a letter
or number (or word or phrase) to the front of the cap as
desired. Double-whammy creative top points can be
scored by cutting out letters in antique fonts from old
magazines, books, newspapers or leaflets. It's also a new
way to learn a language, if you collect printed material
while abroad.

-- **An iron will** --

For readers with a surrealist bent, an old steam iron
– customized according to taste – can make a very
effective doorstop, bookend or sculptural talking point.
Best to remove the wires first.

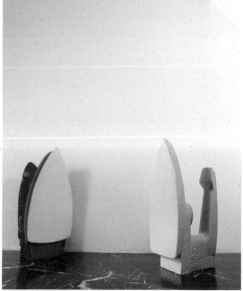

Design example
Maarten de Ceulaer
Iron Bookends

Maarten de Ceulaer was trained in interior and product design at the Saint-Lukas Hogeschool Brussel and the Design Academy Eindhoven. The Iron Bookends were originally just painted steam irons made in collaboration with Julien van Havere for a one-off event at a secondhand shop in Brussels. But when every item sold, the designer decided to develop the line commercially, casting the iron shapes in strong industrial plaster before dipping them in rubber for extra durability.

Design example
Afroditi Krassa
394 Yellow Pages
In an appropriate reappropriation of an old copy of the Yellow Pages phone directory, London-based Afroditi Krassa designed the *394 Yellow Pages* business-card holder. Trimming the massive tome down to a more manageable (although somewhat random) 394 pages before rolling and binding it inside a chrome tube, the resulting object is just as good for displaying photographs, or used as a letter rack.

Design example

Emiliana Design
Raspall
Barcelona-based Emiliana Design produced several ready-made products in the late 1990s, including Raspall, a letter rack that exploits the holding power of a broom-head full of bristles. Emiliana would go on to design chocolates for Enrico Rovira in the form of the city's iconic paving stones, which have become some of Barcelona's bestselling confections.

STEP-BY-STEP

Layer Cake

Cupcakes have exploded in Europe lately. Not literally (except perhaps in the kitchens of some unfortunate would-be chefs) but – like those other Manhattan confections, such as certain brands of glazed donut and particularly vertiginous designer heels – for some reason cupcakes suddenly are everywhere. Which is all well and good, but where to put them all? On a cupcake tower, of course. Make your own. These directions are for a simple, three-tiered stand – but there's no reason you shouldn't get more ambitious. Add as many layers as you have cakes to fill. The plates can be mismatched, but it helps if they are pretty.

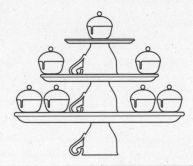

You will need:

_ One large plate
_ One small plate
_ One saucer
_ Three supports – ideas for these include upturned cups, drinking glasses and porcelain figurines
_ Ceramic glue (this is usually dishwasher-proof but check the brand beforehand)
_ Sandpaper

_ Masking tape
_ Paper towel
_ Nail-polish remover
_ Paint (optional, for decorating)
_ Ribbon (optional, for decorating)
_ Pretty paper (optional, for decorating)

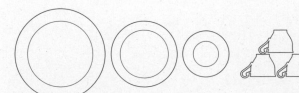
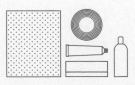

1_ If you are using plates and supports that you need to paint and decorate first (such as terracotta pots) do this first, using your optional decorating equipment.

2_ You are going to glue the layers on top of each other beginning with your strongest and lowest support, followed by the largest plate, and layering the tiers up gradually. Before applying the glue to the dishes, lightly sand both surfaces. Wipe away the dust with a cloth, then coat one edge with glue.

Press the pieces together and clean off any overflow with a paper towel dipped in nail-polish remover.

3_ Apply a weight, such as a book, to clamp the surfaces while the glue sets. This may take three hours or more. Wait for each tier to dry before adding the next. Finish with the saucer on top.

4_ Add cake.

1_

2_

3_

3-4

3-4

3-4

4_

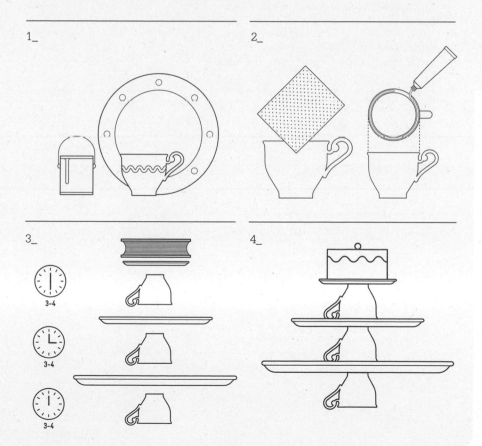

-- Windows applications --

Old CD cases turned inside-out can be put to use as desktop photoframes — especially apt for the home office, where the cases may well have originated. Alternatively it's possible to make a desk calendar in the same way. Cut 12 pieces of card to the same size as a CD inlay and just mark the days of each month on them.

-- Present and correct --

Old magazines can make excellent wrapping paper. Any pages not suitable for the outside of a present can be shredded and usefully used as padding inside it.

-- Patch test --

Découpage — the art of using magazine, comic-book or newspaper cuttings to decorate, papier-mâché style, accessories, walls and items of furniture — has hardly ever been fashionable, for the good reason that it generally looks terrible. But, done with a little panache, it can actually be a novel technique for decorating anything from shoeboxes to mug trees. Rather than cutting out images, try treating the magazines as fabric — cutting out colours and patterns to a diamond template, and assembling the pieces into quilt or pinwheel formations.

-- Bulb airing --

Designers have converted empty incandescent bulbs into oil lamps or novelty salt shakers. To hollow out your own, use a pair of needlenose pliers to grip the solder point at the end of the bulb. Give it a twist to free the brass contact and break one of the wires leading to the filament. Pull out the contact, carefully crack and remove the glass insulator and you should be able to see the inside supports of the filament and the fill tube containing kaolin. Break this using a screwdriver and shake out the filament parts before cleaning out the bulb with a cloth. (Wear gloves to protect your hands in case the bulb breaks, and never try this with a fluorescent bulb: the powder used to coat their insides is toxic.)

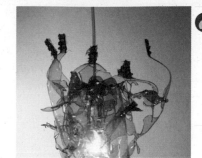

Design example
Johanna Keimeyer
Recycle Lights
Influenced by the Brazilian
Campana brothers, German
artist Johanna Keimeyer
learned to "treat trash like
treasure" and "garbage like gold",
and embarked on a hunt for
packaging that she could use in
her collection of Recycle Lights.
Her search led her across half of
Europe, through Slovenia, Spain,
France, England and Germany.
The result was a collection of
chandeliers, an object she
chose to symbolize beauty
and extravagance.

Design example
Studio Verissimo
Spoon
It has a slightly misleading
name for a chandelier made
from plastic coffee-stirrers,
but Spoon is an elegant take
on the swizzle stick any way
you look at it. Studio Verissimo
is a collaboration between
designers Cláudio Cardoso
and Telma Veríssimo. Both are
from Portugal, where the coffee
stirrers used in most cafes
are typically clear plastic. The
material has many of the same
qualities as crystal, refracting
and reflecting light in the manner
of what traditionalists might
call a "proper" chandelier.

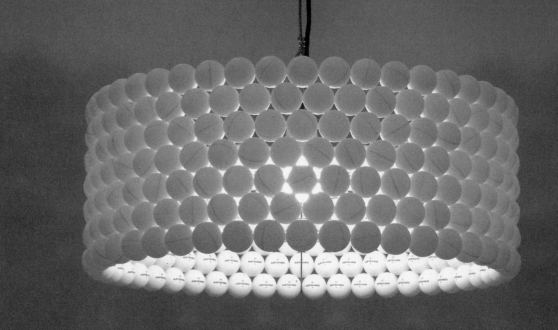

Design example

Diaz Kleefstra
Ping-Pong Ball Lamp
Dutch designer Diaz Kleefstra
used 315 table-tennis balls to
create this pendant lamp in the
spirit of ad-hocism, although the
balls Kleefstra used were new.
The lamp was originally named
after table-tennis champion
Bettine Vriesekoop, but was later
changed due to legal issues.

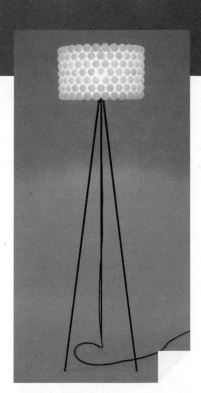

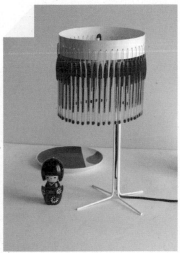

Design example
enPieza!
Volivik Lamps
EnPieza!'s Volivik collection uses the humble BIC ballpoint pen in place of crystals to refract the light. The lamps were a huge hit when a mammoth chandelier version was launched in a limited edition of 30 in 2007. Alongside the paperclip chandelier from JAM, it seems that the office stationery cupboard has never been such a rich source of inspiration.

STEP-BY-STEP

Cut-glass Accents

There was a time, before the 1970s, when fondue sets were not languishing at the
back of the cupboard in every home – used once, and then put 'away'. Forever.
Before fondue sets existed, the back of the cupboard was reserved for the equipment
of other short-lived fads. Such as a glass-cutting kit, maybe. A glass-cutting kit allows
you to make vases, glasses, and all sorts from that stash otherwise destined
for recycling – with no craft apprenticeship or degree in applied arts required.
That said, bear in mind that you'll get better at this with practice, so it's worth trying
it out on a beer bottle before turning that jeroboam from your wedding into
a new cooler. These instructions show how to make a simple vase
from a wine bottle.

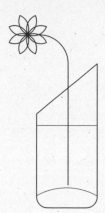

You will need:

_ Glass-cutting kit
_ Candle
_ Ice cubes
_ Glass bottle
_ Sandpaper

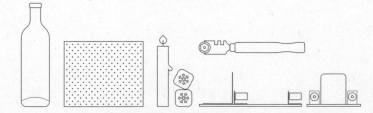

1_ Decide where to cut the bottle and at what angle. If it's your first attempt, opt for a straight cut; as you get more experienced you can try more complicated avant-garde designs.

2_ Place the bottle into the cutter so it lies flat on the rollers. The scoring blade should be positioned over the line you want to cut. Hold the bottle in both hands and slowly roll it towards you, keeping the pressure even as you cut a score-line around the bottle. The cut doesn't need to be especially deep, but it does need to be straight.

3_ Light a candle, and, holding the line you have scored directly above the flame, rotate the bottle slowly so that the score is evenly heated all around.

4_ Next, slide an ice cube along the scored line. You may hear tiny cracking noises; this shows that the process is working.

5_ Repeat Steps 3 and 4 a few times until the bottle breaks cleanly.

6_ Use sandpaper to smooth the cut surfaces of the glass and elimate sharp edges.

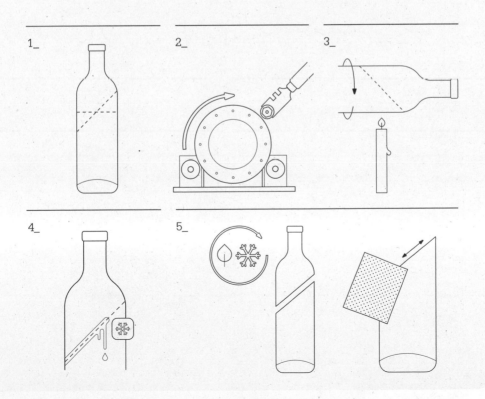

1_

2_

3_

4_

5_

Design example
**Tord Boontje and Emma Woffenden
tranSglass**
The tranSglass project is an
elegant line of tableware made
from recycled wine and beer
bottles from the restaurant
industry. Tumblers, vases, and
carafes are all fashioned through
collecting, cleaning and recutting old glassware into new
shapes. The line is recognized as
a design classic and is included
in the permanent collection at
the Museum of Modern Art in
New York. The Guatemalan fair-
trade manufacturing process
also allows the glassware to
be produced at a low cost.

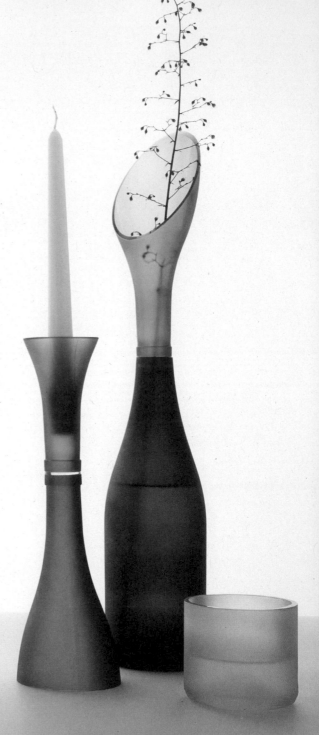

-- Stacking the odds --

Glue hundreds of old CDs together in a big tall stack. Run a cool-burning fluorescent tube light up through the hole in the centre. Cut a groove along the CDs at the bottom of the stack for the wire to pass through. *Voilà*: a slightly bizarre new table lamp.

-- Snakes and ladders --

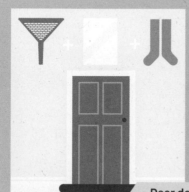

Cut off an old pair of tights at the gusset and fill the legs with sand or rice or polyfill to make a traditional draft stopper. Optional developments for those with the time and inclination might be to tie off a "head" adding eyes, nose and tail to make the draft excluder resemble a sausage dog, or a felt forked tongue for a snake.

-- Deer deer --

It is common to see CDs stuck back-to-back (shiny side out) and hung from trees in rural areas in Europe, particularly in places where deer pose a threat to crops and vegetable patches. As they swing about and catch the light the CDs act as an effective deterrent to hungry furry or feathered trespassers, including pigeons, rabbits, foxes and badgers.

-- Opaque intentions --

Real, fresh flowers are always preferable when they are available, but fake ones do sometimes have their place. Any nimble-fingered crafty type can make superior fake blooms using only some old coloured tights and a bit of wire. To form each petal cut the fabric to size, fold it in half, stretch it over a wire loop and tie it at the ends.

Design example
COMMITTEE
Kebab Lamps
Clare Page and Harry Richardson of COMMITTEE use the assorted crockery, vases, figurines, and other chintzy bric-a-brac that they find in the fly-tips, skips and markets of south-east London to build their Kebab lamps. Far from random, however, each unique construction has been carefully planned to tell a story or explore a theme. The designers were quoted as saying "We'd quite like our work to follow in the footsteps of a Dada sound poem, nodding in passing to the Bauhaus, while wearing some Versace," which says it all.

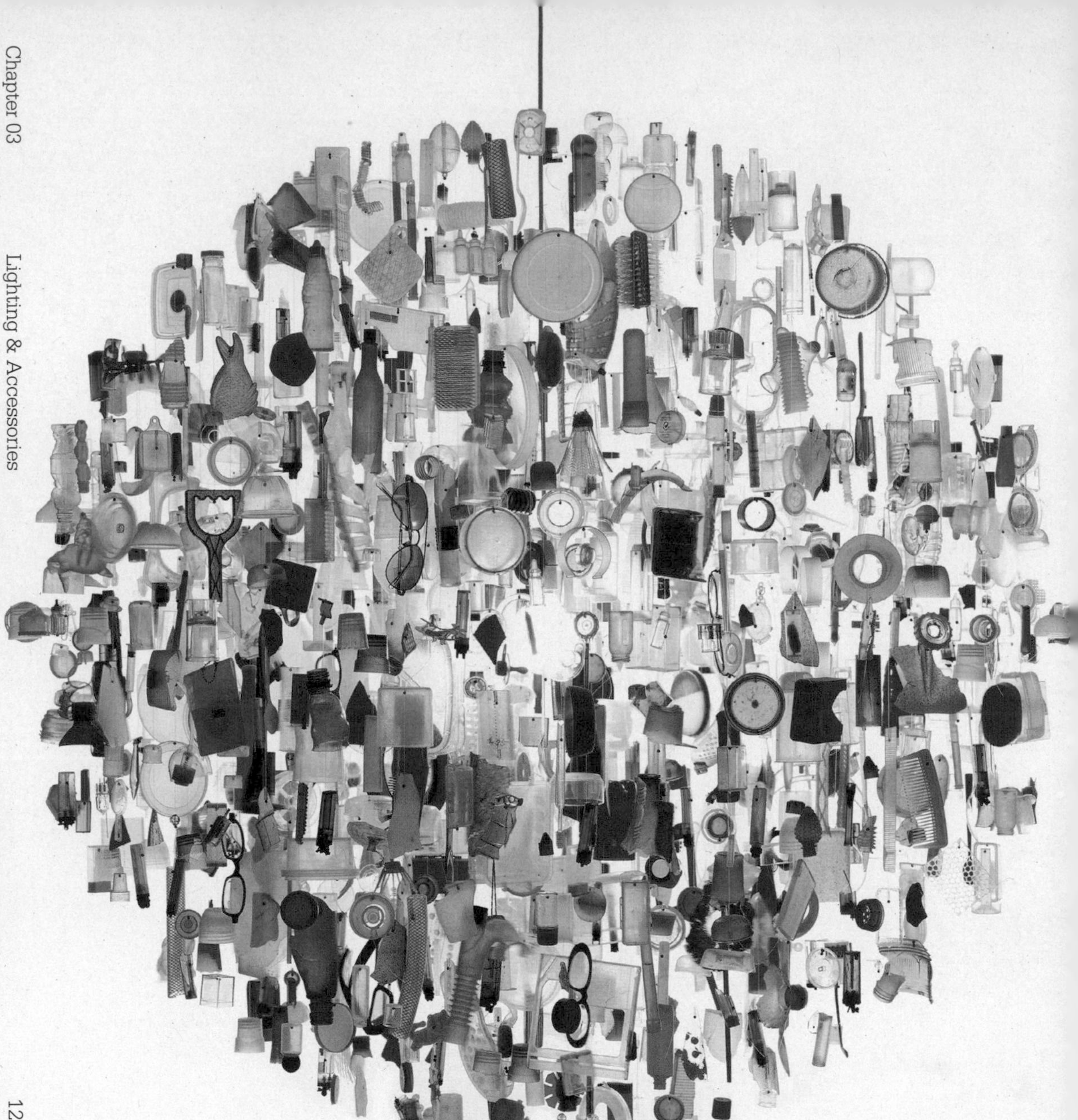

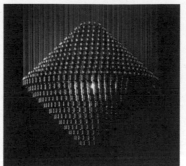

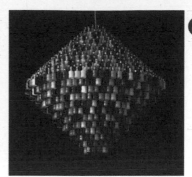

Design example

Stuart Haygarth Chandeliers

Stuart Haygarth's show-stopping chandeliers are built from what he calls "the flotsam and jetsam of everyday life". Collecting the material over many years, Haygarth sorts, categorizes and carefully suspends it *in situ*. The Tide Chandelier is a 1.5-metre wide installation made of plastic debris washed up on a specific stretch of Kent coastline, while other chandeliers use party-popper casings from millenium celebrations, or hundreds of pairs of glasses found through Vision Aid Overseas (a charitable organization for the collection and redistribution of discarded prescription spectacles).

-- Greatest fan --

A large broken electric fan will dismantle into a number of component parts, many of which could prove to be quite useful with little or no adaptation required. The blades, for example, can make fabulous canapé dishes (don't laugh till you've tried it) while the cage might be repurposed as a nice hanging basket.

-- Fruit loose and fancy free --

Put your peaches on a pedestal with a distinctive fruit stand, made from leftover cardboard tubes (the ones that come inside kitchen foil are ideal for this purpose as they are stiffer than those from loo rolls or paper towels). Chop up the tubes into short blocks of varying heights, and bond the cylinders together using double-sided sticky tape. Paint the entire structure in fruity hues and coat with a water-based sealant before letting it dry overnight.

-- Shell shock --

Turn those giant seashells you picked up on that tropical beach (or at the local church jumble sale) into canapé dishes and serving bowls for seafood snacks. Boil the shells thoroughly to sanitize them and remove all sediment first. Serve with a pina colada in a coconut shell.

Design example
Anneke Jakobs
Chiquita Chandelier
Proving, as we've already seen
done with party poppers and
ballpoint pens, that you can
make a chandelier out of pretty
much anything, Dutch designer
Anneke Jakobs creates a light
and fruity version with cardboard
cut-outs of bananas. After
spending more than enough
time snipping out the logos
from Chiquita cartons that
she found around the streets,
Jakobs subsequently decided
to embrace the open-source
nature of reappropriation by
offering a digital manual to make
the chandelier on her website.

Design example
JAM
Paperclip Chandelier
In an installation for a 2003
exhibition at Sotheby's
auction house called Waste
To Taste, JAM designed a room
completely made up of pick-
and-mix sweets, sponsored
by now-defunct general store
Woolworths. With all the candy
it could have dreamed of at its
creative disposal JAM made
clothes, display units, the floor
and the curtains from the
sweets and wrappers. The
firm also painstakingly
constructed a chandelier
out of 50,000 paperclips for
the same exhibition.

-- Not a lotta bottle --

Not so very long ago people would have milk delivered, not in a carton dropped off with their rest of their online supermarket sweep, but in proper glass bottles, with little aluminium caps. The bottles would be left outside the front door by the milkman (unless you left out a little note saying "Not Today Thank You Mr Milkman" if you were going away). You would leave your empties for him to collect at the same time. You would probably also have a little milk-bottle holder to keep the doorstep neat and tidy. But what to do with that now? You can still put bottles in it, but use them as vases, fill them with forget-me-nots, and wallow in nostalgia instead.

-- Baking do --

If you have an old baking tray that has given up the biscuit ghost due to rust, it will still make a magnetic bulletin board for the kitchen where it can be used to pin recipes, notes and coupons. Clean up the tray, dry it, and paint with anti-rust paint. If you don't fancy the rusty rustic look, cover the tray with a piece of scrap fabric, paper or wallpaper. (Note that many baking trays now are made from non-magnetic aluminium, so check before you set to work.) Fasten to the wall, apply magnets, and away you go.

-- Fillet-O-Fish --

Who needs a boring screensaver showing swimming tropical fish when you can have the real thing? A MacQuarum is – as one might imagine – an old Mac monitor repurpoed as a fish tank. It's possible to find lots of helpful instructions online that explain the fundamentals of taking the chips out, and putting the fish in, with inspirational examples to boot. (Or not to boot).

STEP-BY-STEP

STEP-BY-STEP

Magic Lanterns

It's easy to light up the garden on a summer evening by placing tea-light
candles in glass jars and hanging them from trees. Tin cans can also be
recycled in this way: just punch a pattern of little holes in the sides
so that the light can shine through.

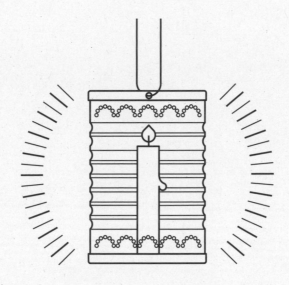

You will need:

- Empty tin cans
- Water
- Pliers
- Freezer
- Medium-sized nail
- Large nail
- Hammer
- String or wire
- Candles

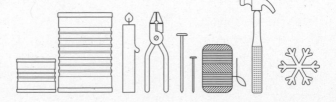

1_ Use a pair of pliers to bend down any sharp edges on the tin cans.

2_ Fill the cans with water and pop them in the freezer.

3_ When the water is frozen (it might need to be left overnight), punch designs in each can using a hammer and the medium-sized nail. The ice is key as it stops the can from denting as you do this.

4_ Use the large nail to make two holes on opposite sides of the rim.

5_ After the ice has melted, thread some string or wire through the large holes to form a handle.

6_ Put the candle inside the can and bask in the glow of your handiwork.

1_

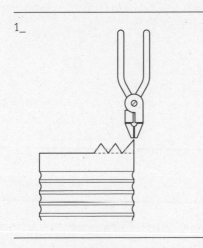

2_

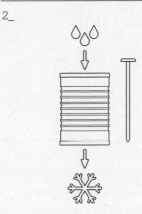

3_

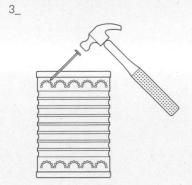

5_

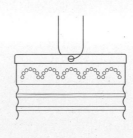

-- Back to black --

Blackboard paint is the remaker's secret weapon: anything you can paint with it, you can turn into a blackboard. (Blackboard paint is as versatile as emulsion in coating different surfaces effectively.) Some objects will work better as blackboards than others: an old chopping board is easier to write on than a flowerpot, and the back of a cupboard door is going to be more appropriate than the front of the front door, unless you're after an especially novel take on the visitors' book.

-- Brightest whites --

Large plastic packaging items – for example, those gigantic bottles of washing detergent – can be turned into kitsch but practical lampshades. Cut a hole in the side of the bottle to run the wire through, and a larger hole at the bottom so that you can affix the bulb inside (make sure it is cool-burning and doesn't touch the plastic sides). Depending on the opacity of the bottle, an optional decorative touch would be to punch small holes in the shade to let the light shine through.

-- Mug shot --

With their easy disposability and screw-on lids, glass jars make handy 'to-go' cups when you're in a hurry to get somewhere and haven't finished your coffee. The lid is far more effective at preventing spillage than the usual plastic take-out affairs when in a car or on bumpy transport. To keep the glass from cracking, allow boiling liquids to cool slightly before filling the jar. A strip of corrugated cardboard or old towel wrapped around the jar will shield your hands from the heat.

-- Cut out and keep --

Wash the coloured plastic packaging from toiletries or detergents and cut it into flat circles. Large disks can be used as makeshift coasters; smaller pieces can be fashioned into tiny lampshades for strings of Christmas lights. Cut a line into the centre of each plastic circle. Just inside one side of the line, cut a slot. Cut the other edge into a tab that will fit the slot, to create a mechanism that allows the plastic to be secured in a cone shape around each bulb.

Design example
Rita Botelho
Salt and Pepper Shakers

Photographic film canisters are reappropriated into salt and pepper shakers in this concept from Portugese product designer Rita Botelho. Picnic-proof and dishwasher-proof in a way that traditional wooden mills are not, the canisters are made of LDPE and HDPE (low density and high density polyethylene), which happen to be two of the most commonly used plastics in food packaging anyway.

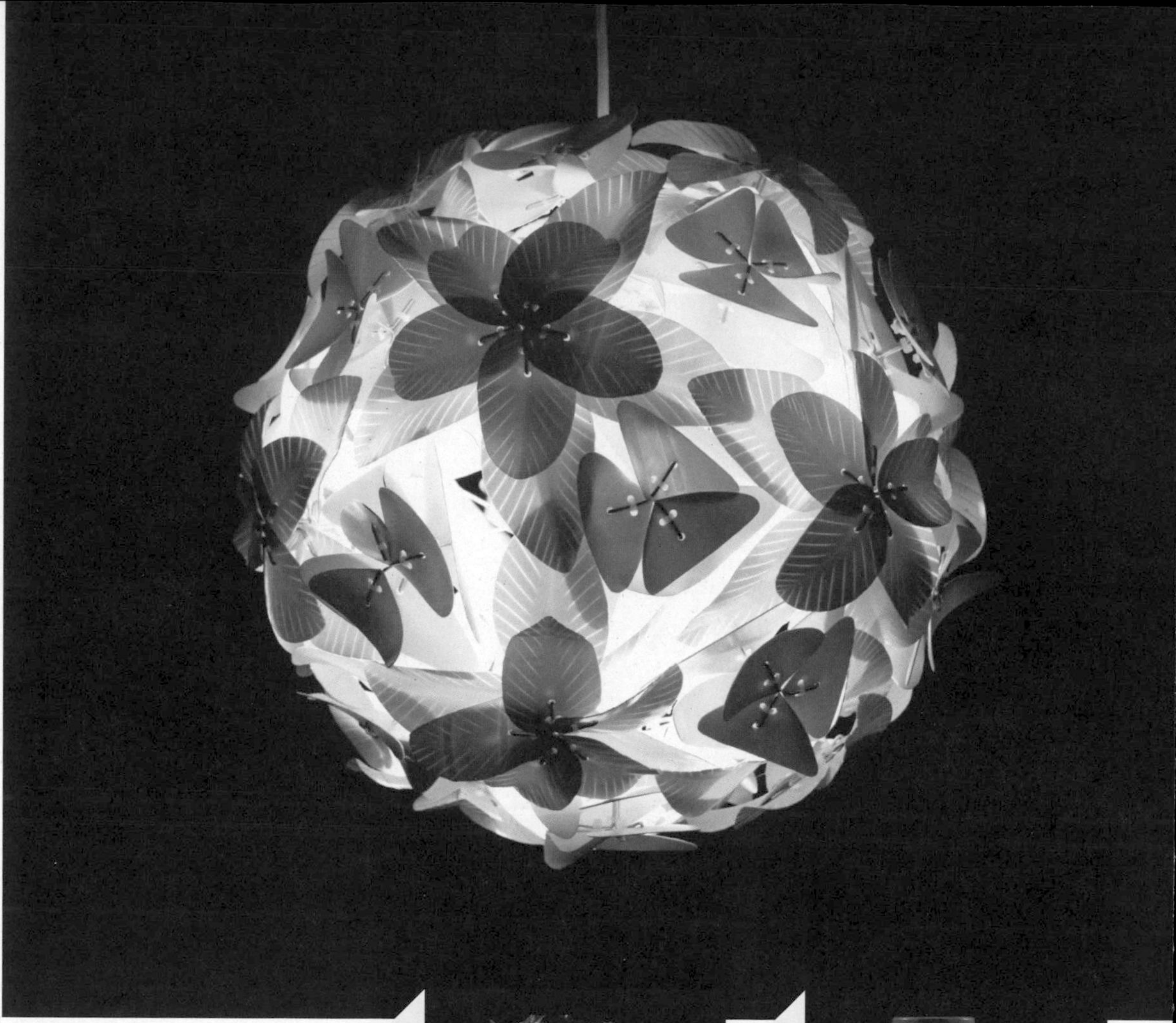

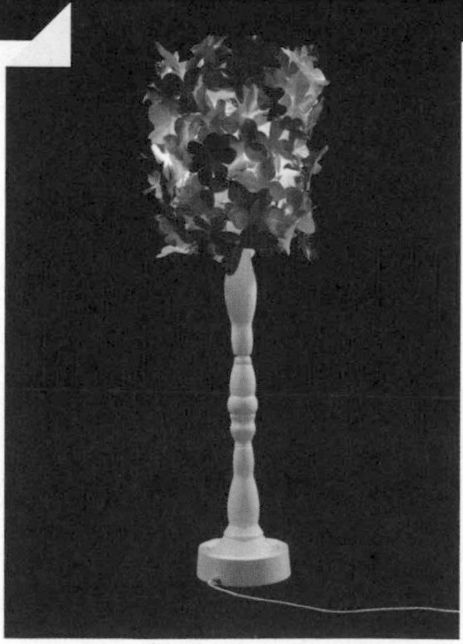

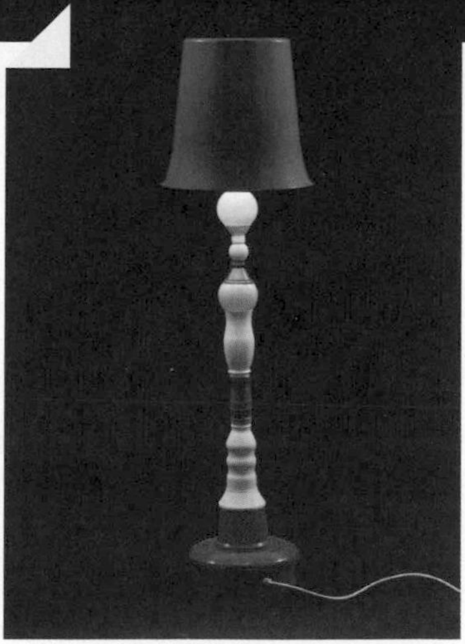

Design example
Heath Nash
Green Lighting

Many of South African sculptor Heath Nash's designs see scavenged plastic packaging transformed into unrecognizable new objects. Having obtained and washed the packaging (often bottles), Nash cuts each item to form a plastic sheet, removing the tops, bottoms and any handles. Next, leaves and flowers are punched out of the sheet with a hammer and a blade attached to a piece of wood. Finally, creases are created by hand. Nash uses the resulting forms as modular elements for lamps, screens and artworks.

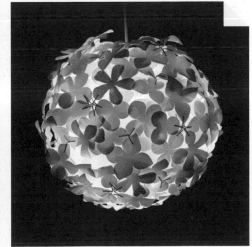

-- Wheelie bins --

The hardwearing, heavy and waterproof properties of rubber make tyres exceptionally useful in the garden. Reappropriating tyres as planters is traditional to the point of being an ironic design classic. Use a single tyre as a raised bed for lettuce or herbs. Alternatively, stack a few tyres on top of each other to make deep potato bins or a composting area.

--Plumb pudding --

Add some industrial chic to your dinner table by constructing tall candle holders using off-the-shelf plumbing parts. It's like Lego, but instead of little plastic bricks you have lead plumbing pipes, flanges, and couplings – all of which can be arranged in whatever order you deem to be most fitting. Start by screwing the pipe into the flange to create the base, and improvise from there.

-- Cover charge --

Vintage magazines, comics and large-format slim paperbacks are often the ideal size to make placemats. They can be used as-is – providing optional inter-course reading material during less successful dinner parties – or laminated with clear plastic to keep the covers protected from spills.

-- Preworn lather --

Packaging can lend itself to as many different uses as there are types of packaging. Fruit from a supermarket is often sold in plastic containers with holes for drainage – perfect for a second life as a soap dish. Mobile-phone packing might also be suitable for the same purpose, and often the plastic is sturdier. Add feet for better drainage by gluing sections of cork to the base.

Design example
Karen Ryan
Second Hand and Unmade 07
Having scoured antiques shops
and markets for plates and
vases, London-based Karen Ryan
files down their glazed surfaces
leaving only stenciled traces
of the original patterns in the
form of words and other motifs.
Her Second Hand series of
plates and Unmade 07 series of
vases are early examples of this
technique. Recycling is central
to Ryan's work and she has
said that she finds it difficult to
watch the news and then design
"yet another superfluous object".

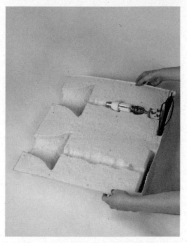

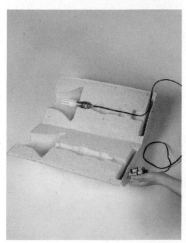

Design example
David Gardner
Packaging Lamp
The Packaging Lamp, designed
by UK-based David Gardner,
uses a handmade paper-pulp
structure both as packaging to
house the bulb plug wire and
socket and as the product itself.
The user removes the electronic
parts and repositions them back
inside the preformed box in the
correct alignment, creating
a functional lamp without
waste packaging.

Design example
Paul Cocksedge
Styrene
One day while, presumably,
he had little else on, British
lighting designer Paul Cocksedge
made the discovery that if a
polystyrene cup is put in the
oven and cooked, it warps,
shrinks and hardens, with a
resulting texture and properties
that are not unlike ceramic.
Armed with this new knowledge
Cocksedge designed the Styrene
lamp, and subsequently won
several awards.

Design example
**Maxim Velcovsky
Catastrophy**
Czech ceramicist Maxim
Velcovsky slip-cast these
apparently traditional forms
in porcelain before spending
some time adding the clay, dust
and found pieces. Many of the
vases also incorporate a number
of Velcovsky's own personal
belongings.

-- Poly morphic --

The polystyrene-block packaging that keeps many electronic devices snug in their boxes when sold can be reused to make all manner of desktop equipment. Carve out the necessary niches with a utility or craft knife to form mobile-phone cradles, cable tidies, drawing-pin cushions and laptop stands.

-- Left wing --

Old mirrors can be repurposed as dishes for canapés, keys or soap if they are still attractive enough for display. Even the wing-mirror of a vintage car – assuming the car is no longer roadworthy or has new wings itself – can be screwed into a bathroom wall, mirror-side up, and used as a space-saving soap holder.

-- Glitter bug --

Novelty windchimes aren't the only use for old CDs – thankfully. Make full use of their shiny surfaces and reappropriate Lionel Richie's greatest hits back into their original disco context by fashioning unwanted CDs into a glitter ball. Cut the CDs into small squares and triangles, and glue them (label side down) onto a large spherical object, such as an old beach ball. Hang it up. Set the lights. And get down.

-- Food fight --

One of the best reuses of board games – especially the classics such as Scrabble, Monopoly and Snakes & Ladders – is to use the boards as placemats. While it might encourage the kids to play with their food, adults might also be tempted into an after-dinner game. Along the same lines, Twister mats can double up as great kitchen tablecloths or picnic mats.

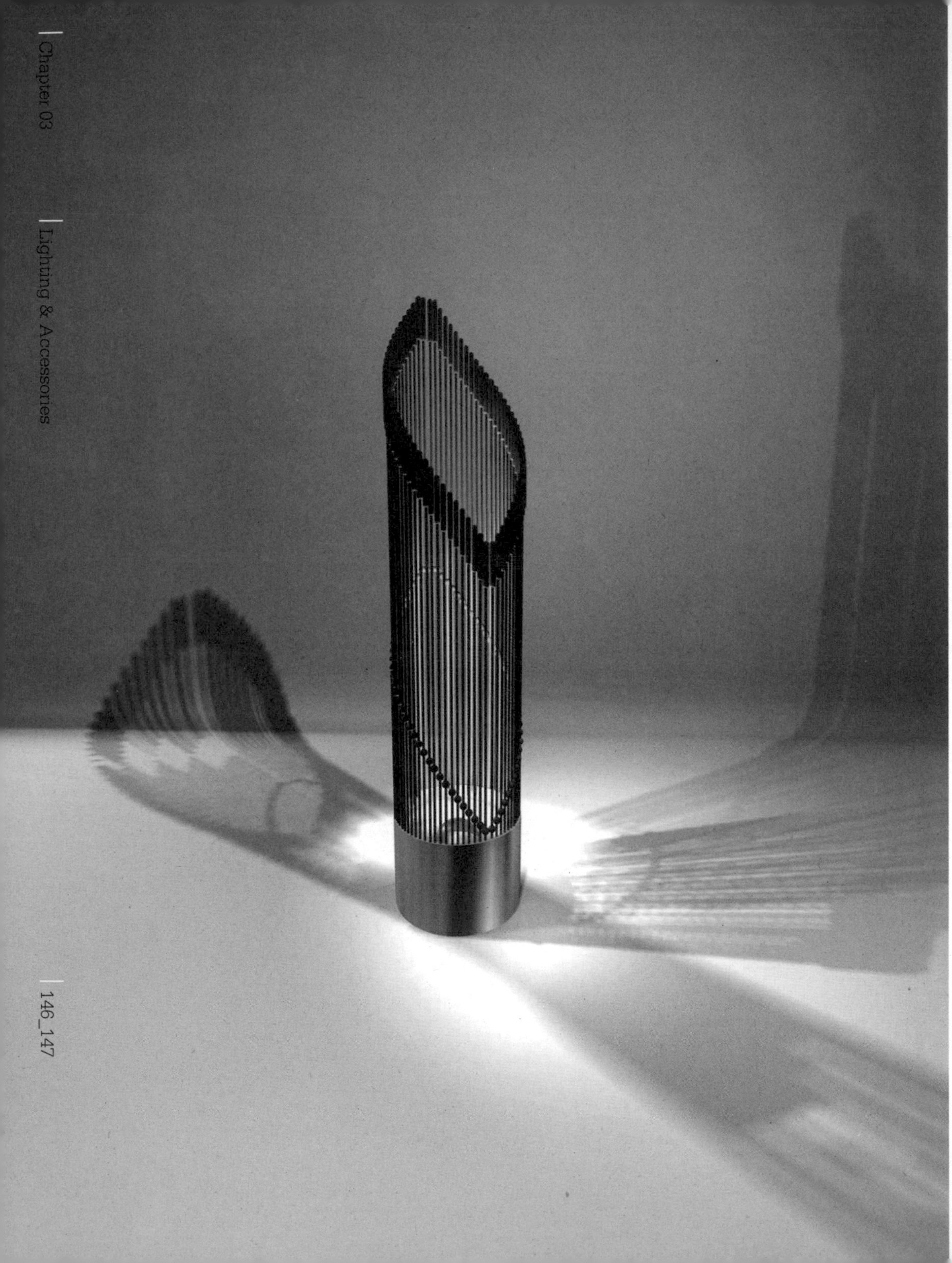

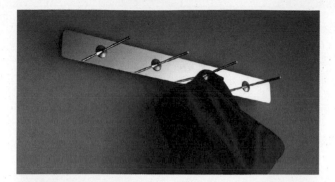

JAM
Audi

In a branding project for car marque Audi, JAM created a television, print and poster campaign that showed Audi car components transformed into a series of household items. A cylinder block became a wine rack, and a spring was adapted into a stylish magazine rack. More innovative still were a toilet-roll holder fashioned from a wing-mirror and wall lights created from the car's hubcaps and petrol-tank cap.

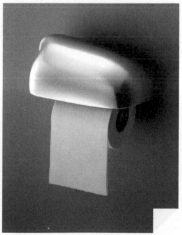

Design example
Junktion
Gas Baskets and Scoop
Colourful metal gas canisters
are cut away, upturned and lined
with rubber to form unusual,
but covetable rustic baskets
and scoops designed and
manufactured by Junktion.

-- Bottle out --

In a fitting balance of supply-and-demand the list of things you can make from an empty wine bottle are seemingly endless. For tealights, use a glass-cutting tool and cut off the base of the bottle to create a shallow dish about two or three centimeters tall, and get rid of the sharp edges either by sanding them down with a file or sandpaper, or by folding tape or a wide rubber band (bicycle inner tubes are perfect) over the rim. For a pair of simple candlesticks to hold tall candles, cut the tops off two bottles, or arrange them spout-to-spout and strap together with duct tape (or inner tubing) for a single, more elaborate version.

-- Spout time --

No need to discard a teapot if the spout gets knocked off. Just fill it with soil and plant one of the trailing varieties of plants and you have a decorative pot, which can be lifted by the handle and watered down the spout.

-- Shady business 1 --

Keep your food in the shade to deter flies in hot weather. Literally. An old lampshade that you no longer want in (or over) the limelight can be repurposed as a food cover. Puns aside, fix some mesh over the open top of the lampshade (or just drape a napkin over it). Place the cover over plates of food to keep off the insects when eating outdoors.

-- Shady business 2 --

A redundant lampshade can also be used upside-down as a wastepaper basket, as a display bowl for potted plants or, if you're a potpourri sort of person, to hold some potpourri. Remove the finial and close up the small end with some card, cork or similar, held down with a bit of superglue.

Design example
Ryan McElhinney
Gold Toy series
Ryan McElhinney's handmade
Gold Toy lamp and mirror were
designed to make use of all
the lost toys of London. Rather
than ending their little lives in
a landfill, McElhinney bonded
the toys together and then
coated them in a high gloss
polyurethane lacquer.

TEXTILES & SOFT FURNISHINGS

Bedding, throws, cushions, curtains, rugs, towels, tablecloths and napkins

-- Rice above it --

For those who bulk-buy rice, the sturdy cloth sacks – which are often printed with exotic graphics – can be stuffed to make floor cushions. Shredded paper makes a good filler because the heavy-duty fabric disguises lumps and bumps. The end result is a weighty, satisfying and stable seat.

-- Lap of luxury --

If a cotton or linen tablecloth has had its day, chances are that it will still make a number of good napkins. Mark out squares slightly larger than a standard napkin size on the good areas of the tablecloth, cut them out and hem the edges.

-- Feather bluster --

If feather cushions and pillows become heavy and lumpy over time, they can be revived with a standard bicycle pump. Insert the nozzle into a small hole in the pillow or cushion case and after a few pumps the air will have circulated and loosened up the contents. The result? A pillow that could be mistaken for a cloud.

-- Speculative bubble --

There are so many things to do after moving into a new home – and many of them you will want to do with a certain degree of privacy – so before anything else you're going to need curtains. However, if the ones you packed are still somewhere at the bottom of a box, just use the bubble wrap from the top of another box. Fix it temporarily to the windows for a covering that lets light in while being opaque enough to keep nosey new neighbours at bay.

Design example
Freitag

Since 1993, brothers and graphic designers Markus and Daniel Freitag have been manufacturing bags and other accessories such as keytags and iPod cases from old truck tarpaulin, seat belts and bicycle inner tubes. Initially conceived to meet the brothers' own need for hardwearing waterproof products that would survive the rain as they cycled around their native Switzerland, the Frietag line was an immediate hit that would go on to be sold (and copied) internationally.

Design example
Denise Bird
Iceland Bath Cushions

In 2005, Denise Bird established her company, Denise Bird Woven Textiles (DBWT) in Wiltshire, England, to research and develop ecological fabrics. Working in collaboration with fair-trade registered manufacturers, Bird usually uses organic cotton to make scarves, wraps and ponchos. Standing out among the collection, however, is a series of bath cushions made using supermarket plastic bags.

-- Crafty shopper --

Every household hoards plastic bags in abundance, but some households seem to get through more than others. When there are enough bags available, and if you are craftily inclined, it is possible to make plastic fabric by stripping up the bags and weaving the strips through fruit nets (such as those used to hold oranges).

-- Holy sheet --

Household linen being as scarce as everything else in wartime Britain, families stretched to their last threadbare sheets were urged to make them go a little bit further using what became known as the "Sides-to-Middle" technique. When a sheet became thin and worn in the middle, it would be cut in half lengthwise and the halves sewn back together so that the worn parts were reversed on the edges and the good parts in the centre. If you want to try the technique, make sure the new seam is as flat as possible so you don't encounter any bumps in the night.

-- Warming signs --

Microwaveable heating pads are one of the most satisfying ways to use up a few scraps of cotton fabric and some uncooked rice. To make hot little pillows that will keep your mitts warm in winter and your toes toasty at the end of the bed, sew up a simple cloth bag (any shape and size you need as long as it fits in the microwave) and fill it with the rice. If you really hate sewing, you can use an old sock and tie a knot in it – but it won't be as comforting as a soft fluffy towelling version made with love and care. Alternative fillings include wheat, barley, oatmeal and cherry pits, while some people also add spices, herbs and essential oils to the mix for a more aromatherapeutic result. Place in microwave and heat for 1 to 3 minutes, depending on the size of bag – and remember only to use cotton fabrics – synthetics might melt and get a little messy. The bags can also be kept in the freezer and used as a cooling pad or freezer pack in case you run out of peas in an emergency.

Design example

Ellie Evans
Hanging pockets
UK-based Ellie Evans combines traditional hand embroidery with digital print to create custom-made textile pieces – from pincushions to document wallets. Exploring heritage and identity in her work, one of Evans's specialities is her "hanging pocket" a nostalgic but functional keepsake dating from Victorian times. Originally women would wear a hanging pocket around the waist between the skirt and the petticoats to provide a private and safe place for personal possessions. Evans's contemporary versions can be displayed around the home or worn in the style of a handbag.

Design example
Kate Goldsworthy

British textile designer Kate
Goldsworthy is inspired by light
and transparency and makes
much use of recycled elements
in her dynamic fabrics for the
interior market. With academic
training in Textile Futures at
Central Saint Martins College
of Art and Design, Goldsworthy's
commissions include a set
of sheer window panels for
a London restaurant, fabric
screens and wall hangings
for private collections, and
a collection of little black
dresses made from recycled
post-consumer synthetic
waste materials.

Design example
**Catherine Hammerton
Victoriana**
Textile designer Catherine Hammerton uses techniques such as traditional silk-screen printing, hand-stitching and collage on all sorts of "found" fabric and paper materials, which are sourced at antique fairs across Europe. Victoriana, for example, is a collection of hand-printed papers delicately embellished with stitched lace and paper birds.

STEP-BY-STEP

Tuft Love

Tufting is an easy way to reinvigorate an old sofa or armchair that has become
a bit slouchy. Not only does it reintroduce some bounce to upholstery that has got
saggy in its old age, but it can add a fashionable update to scatter cushions too.
For the uninitiated it's worth mentioning that there are many different types
of tufting and this (the simplest by a long way) is not recommended for leather
sofas or for diamond tufting.

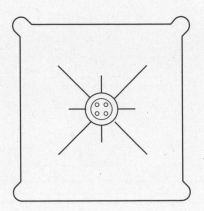

You will need:

- Upholstery thread
- Chalk
- Ruler
- Upholstery needle
  (straight and long)
- Scissors
- Buttons (optional)

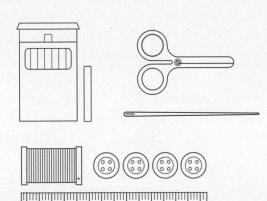

1_ Make sure you start with freshly cleaned cushions as you'll need to unpick the stitches in order to remove the covers when you want to wash them later. Then, take the cushion to be tufted and fluff it vigorously.

2 Measure (with the ruler) and mark (with the chalk) where you want your tufts to be. A single stitch will do for a scatter cushion, but for a back pad you might want to add up to four.

3_ Thread the needle with the upholstery thread and keeping hold of the end, push the needle through the cushion at the marked location and out through the other side.

4_ Remove the needle and re-thread it again with the thread at the front side of the cushion.

5_ Push the needle through the cushion again about a centimetre away from the first insert. If you are using buttons – which distribute the stress better and help prevent the fabric from ripping – add a button here.

6_ Pull the thread through firmly, but not too tightly. Tie the ends off at the back of the cushion and cut away the excess.

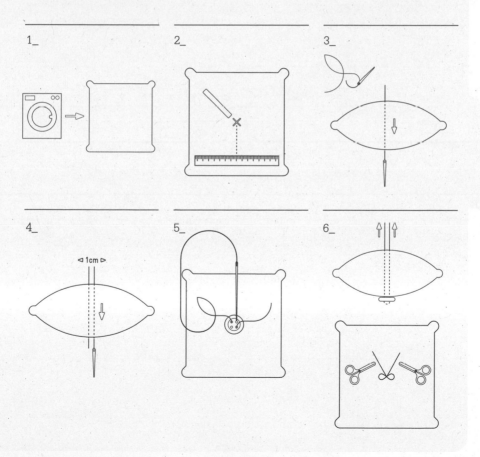

1_

2_

3_

4_

⊲ 1cm ⊳

5_

6_

-- Square roots --

To shorten an old pillowcase to make a cushion cover, turn it inside out and stitch across the closed end to make a square. Trim off the excess and add buttons, ribbons and pompoms as you see fit.

-- Clean cut case --

Convert old pillowcases into laundry bags by adding a drawstring around the opening. A matched pair of old cases will give you a matched set of bags (for separating light and dark loads). If the bags are not overfilled, they can be loaded straight into the washing machine to protect delicate items while washing.

-- Stick in the mud --

Old seagrass floor matting that is worn out in places can be cut down to size and adapted to make internal doormats wherever mud tracking poses a problem. If the will is there, canvas ribbon stitched around the edges makes the most appropriate trim, but isn't strictly necessary.

-- Light showers --

Recycle an old shower curtain into damp-proof coverings for picnics and other messy projects: tablecloths, bibs, mats and placemats can be easily cut out of the good bits. Mucky pups might also benefit from a little section placed underneath their food bowl.

-- Regain bounce --

A quick method of refluffing pillows or duvets is to run them through the dryer with three clean tennis balls. Meanwhile, if an old feather duvet or quilt is wearing at the seams and leaking feathers, take out the feathers, wash them and use them to stuff a new cover or a few pillows. To wash the feathers, secure them in two pillowcases before putting them in the washing machine. Tumble dry thoroughly to prevent the feathers from getting mouldy.

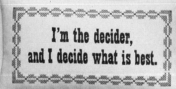

Design example
Margaret Cusack

New York illustrator Margaret Cusack uses stitches and fabric to create sought-after hangings, sculptures and props utilizing intense colour, texture, and detail. Using machine-appliqué and hand embroidery, Cusack's artwork adorns everything from greeting cards to postage stamps. Cusack often works on a large scale to make posters and wall coverings in fabric. In 1988, Cusack received the Alumni Achievement Award from the Pratt Institute of Art in New York City in recognition of her new take on the craft of the quilt.

Design example
Jo Meesters
TESTLAB
In 2008 Jo Meesters created TESTLAB, a series of research experiments into the possibilities of discarded materials. The first project to be realized, entitled "Odds & Ends, Bits & Pieces", was a collection made from 34 old wooden beams reconstructed into 4 furniture pieces that would then be upholstered using 16 secondhand blankets woven together.

Design example
Galya Rosenfeld
Modular Series
San Francisco-based Galya Rosenfeld created the Modular Series using reclaimed ultrasuede scraps from the upholstery industry. Reconstructing the fabric using interlocking puzzle-shaped pieces, Rosenfeld then used it to make cushions, slippers, scarves and throws, among other items. All her pieces are handmade individually, often substituting crafty engineering tricks in place of thread, patterns and other traditional tailoring methods.

Design example
NIIMI
Towel With Further Options
Beginning with the idea of cutting
down a towel to extend its lifetime,
Japanese designers NIIMI created
the Towel With Further Options.
A grid-like pattern is woven into
the towel and acts as a marker to
show how the user could cut the
towel down (without fraying) into
a bathmat and cleaning rags as it
wears out. Although the practice
of cutting down towels is universal
NIIMI is specifically referencing
the Japanese tradition of cutting
up old *yukata* (Japanese bathing
clothes) to make nappies or floor
cloths. When the towel won a
design award from Muji, the judges
praised NIIMI's knowledge of the
production processes involved in
making towels, as often a factory-
manufactured washcloth is made
from a large piece of towel divided
into smaller pieces.

-- Old wise towel --

Build your own bathmat using old towels and/or T-shirts. Wash the fabric well and use scissors to cut it into little strips of about 10 cm by 2 cm. Next, find a suitably sized piece of gridded matting (available in craft stores if you don't have any around the house), and knot each strip of fabric along the grid, making sure that all the knots and tufted ends all face the same way.

-- Hot towel --

Worn-out bath towels can be cut up and hemmed to make small kitchen towels. Alternatively, they can also be constructed into a useful pad for handling hot pans and plates. Cut the towel into small squares and stack up three or four together. Sew a pocket of the same size from any other scrap fabric you like the look of, and pad it with the towels before stitching up the end. Quilt it by running the sewing machine across the end result.

-- Blind nice --

If the end has fallen off the string from a window blind, it can be quickly fixed using a bead from a broken necklace. A plastic thimble (such as those found in Christmas crackers) is also a good solution: poke a hole in the top, run the string through it and tie a knot. The knot will be hidden in the thimble.

-- The towel and the pussycat --

Fluffier members of the household will often appreciate old towels even when they seem threadbare to everyone else. Keep them to use as pet blankets and pet bed liners, and fold them up into little pet pillows.

-- Power nappy --

Just as there is no end to the list of thrifty uses you can find for attractive scraps of fabric, there is no end to the options for used-a-few-times terrycloth nappies either. Boiled and reused again and again, and passed on to umpteen children, they will keep on going for a lifetime as floor cloths and dusters, or rags for cleaning paintbrushes.

STEP-BY-STEP

Pocket change

- - - - - - - - - - - - - - - - - -

While this instructional is a very useful way to transform an old pillowcase into
a peg bag, it has to be acknowledged that a household usually will only need
one peg bag in service at any one time. If you call it a chair pocket, however,
it has a whole lot more potential: perfect for holding and organizing books,
magazines, remote controls and reading glasses, they can be used by
the side of a bed, in a study or sewing room to keep supplies handy, or even
in the kitchen. For a variation, leave the magazine out and add ties either side
to wear around your waist as a utility apron.

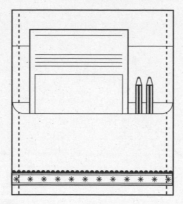

You will need:

- Pillowcase
- Scissors
- Sewing machine and thread
- Magazine
- Decorative trim (optional)

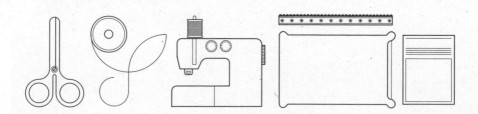

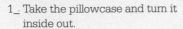

1_ Take the pillowcase and turn it inside out.

2_ Stitch up each side from the bottom edge to the top to until you have the desired width. You may not need to do this if you want it pillowcase width to begin with. Cut off the excess.

3_ Turn the pillowcase right side out again and fold up the open end up towards the closed end.

4_ Cut the side seams of the open end to the length of the cuff and sew down the folded flaps to create two pockets.

5_ On the opposite side of the pillowcase cut a slit large enough to slip an old magazine inside. This will weight the pocket down as it hangs over the side of the chair, or fit inbetween the bed and mattress as a bed pocket.

6_ Decorate to please.

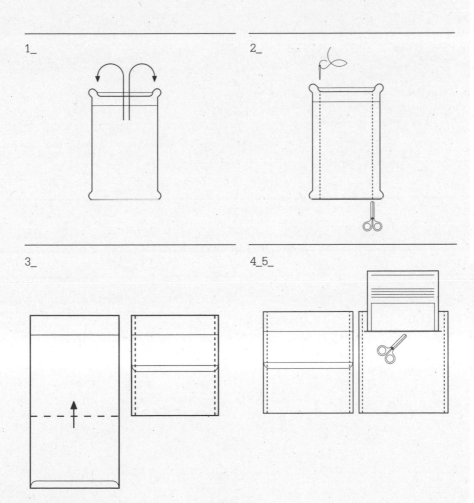

1_

2_

3_

4_5_

-- Ultimate cover-up --

Use larger pieces of scrap fabric (old sheets, curtains or duvet covers work well) to make covers for plastic stacking crates in the bathroom or home office. Not only does it make the crates look lovelier, but the covers can be removed for washing and the crates can still be stacked efficiently.

-- Stamp collecting --

Small stains and flaws in fabric that might otherwise be perfectly serviceable can often be covered up using one or a combination of cleverly placed embroidery, patches, darning or appliqué. But if the idea of cross-stitch, ironic or not, offends your personal style, another option is to use fabric paints, which can be applied with a homemade rubber stamp. Using a utility or craft knife, carve your design of choice into a rubber eraser (if the design includes any letters, draw them in reverse), apply an even coat of paint to the raised surface of the stamp using a brush, stamp the material to be printed and apply a firm, even pressure to realize the image.

-- Heaven scent --

A vintage tablecloth or napkin set, once holey and stained, can be cut down into pretty scraps that are perfect for making lavender bags. An ancient craft from several generations ago, there is no more nostalgic (or effective) way to keep your undies fresh in their drawer, and friends and relatives sweet on their birthdays.

-- Runner marathon --

Remnants of scrap fabric that aren't big enough for a full tablecloth can still make attractive table runners and give the same effect. One of the most underrated staples of formal table dressing, runners have multitudinous functions. If you've had to push two tables together to seat more guests than usual, a table runner can hide the join. Placed crossways across a long table, runners can double up as placemats to be shared by those sitting opposite each other.

Design example
Clara Vuletich
Love & Thrift
Clara Vuletich is a London-based textile designer whose hand-printed textiles and wallpapers are created using traditional methods and – more often than not – recycled materials. When invited to create new work for an exhibition exploring the upcycling of textiles organized by Chelsea College of Art & Design in 2008, Vuletich made Love & Thrift, a project in which she used recycled PVC to coat old textiles such as vintage tablecloths to protect them, before fashioning some into garments. In the same exhibition Vuletich also showed a collection of pre-loved textiles that were overprinted and embroidered to renew their appeal.

Design example
Tal R
Patchwork Eggs
The classic Arne Jacobsen Egg
chair, usually upholstered in leather,
underwent a transformation in 2008
under the direction of artist Tal R.
Commissioned by Fritz Hansen, the
chair's manufacturer, to celebrate
its 50th anniversary, Tal R created
50 unique patchwork designs for
the chairs before giving them each
a new name inspired by the writings
of Sigmund Freud. The Egg, says the
artist, is also a symbol of the forces
of reproduction and the ability to
create new life. Freud's wife Martha,
his early "Irma" dream, and Adler,
the psychologist's close friend and
medical doctor all feature. The chairs
use textiles sourced from around
the world, from those bought in
secondhand shops in Denmark
to washed-out work clothes from
an Israeli kibbutz.

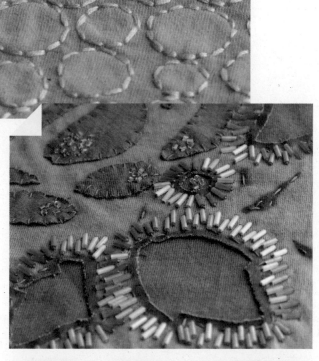

Design example
Alabama Chanin

In 2000, Natalie Chanin, who had been a costume designer for 22 years, established her company in her hometown of Florence, Alabama. Dedicated to environmentally-friendly textiles, Alabama Chanin's limited-edition products use a combination of recycled materials and those handmade by local artisans. The designs for the interiors textiles are inspired by the regional landscape and feature simple graphic patterns picked out in embroidery and appliqué. Alabama Chanin also reupholsters items of found furniture.

STEP-BY-STEP

Choose your rag

One of the most basic craft traditions there is, rag rugs have been made, used and loved for generations, all over the world. There are hundreds of different ways to make them, and the results range from simple hearth-warming dog-mats to exemplary artworks to be passed through generations. Practical and personal, and most originally created out of necessity, they require only the most limited of material supplies and the simplest tools.

You will need:

_ Scrap fabric
_ Scissors
_ Needle and strong thread

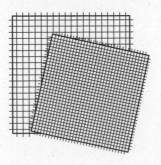

1_ Firstly choose the fabrics that you will use to make your rag rug. Think about the colours and textures with the rug's final use and placement in mind. Cut or tear the material into 5 7 cm strips (bear in mind thinner fabrics should be cut wider than thicker fabrics to ensure a uniform look to the end result.)

2_ Sew the strips together by placing them together at right angles and then sewing them diagonally across the resulting square. Cut the excess material to get rid of any bulkiness and increase seam strength.

3_ For a square or rectangular rug create a number of strips about 30 per cent longer than your desired final rug size. The strips are to be plaited and then laced together in lines. For a round or oval rug, you will be coiling up the plait, so likewise determine the size of the strips accordingly. You can always add more fabric to the strips as you plait if need be.

4_ Attach the strips you have made to a steady base such as a doorknob or bedpost, and plait them. Any number of strands may be used, but generally the more you use, the more robust the end result is likely to be. When the strip of braid is finished, cut off any excess material and tie the ends.

5_ Using a thick lacing thread or string, sew the plaits together at a diagonal until you reach the end of the strip. Turn the rug and return to the opposite end, lacing it in shoelace fashion.

6_ Cut the ends of each row evenly for a rectangular rug and tack them together. For an oval rug, tuck the end neatly under the rug and lace into place.

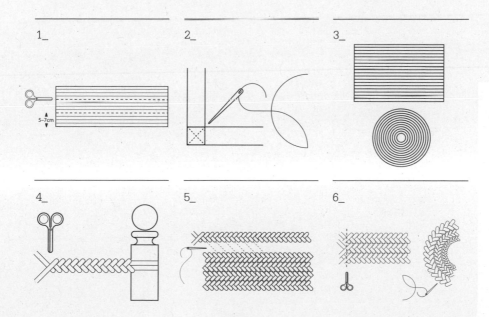

1_

5–7cm

2_

3_

4_

5_

6_

Design example
Huda Baroudi and Maria Hibri
Alef

The Al-Sabah Art & Design Collection is a contemporary gallery established by Kuwait's Sheikh of Chic, Majed Al-Sabah. Launched in 2008 with the mission to promote the craftsmanship of the Middle East and encourage local governments to better preserve their cultural heritage, the first collection was named "Alef" (Arabic for "A"), and included a range by Lebanese designers Huda Baroudi and Maria Hibri. The pair sourced vintage furniture from Europe and Scandinavia and reupholstered the pieces using traditionally embroidered Middle Eastern fabrics.

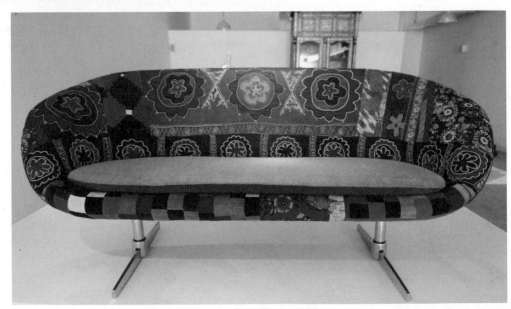

Design example

**Jo Meesters and
Marije van der Park**
Dutch designers Jo Meesters
and Marije van der Park
constructed this carpet in
2005 using discarded woollen
blankets in floral patterns
before adorning it with
traditional needlework.

-- Strip joint --

Scraps of satin, silk and other thin or delicate fabrics can be sliced up to make ribbons. The resulting strips can then be woven together into new textiles, plaited and used for curtain tie-backs, or used as decorations for a pillow, cushion or charismatic hat.

-- Skin graft --

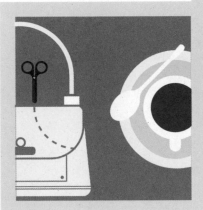

Leather left-over after the death of a handbag can be saved and dissected into coasters, while larger pieces might make useful placemats. A really large scrap – say, from an old sofa or armchair – might cut down to form a protective cover for a writing desk or small table. Leather can easily be shaped or flattened by soaking it in water overnight and reforming it by hand with the help of a mould. Allow it to harden thoroughly before removing it from the mould.

-- Curtain call 1 --

Hide away ugly shelving or cupboards by making a curtain from scrap fabric to hang on the front. It's a neat solution to protect the contents from dust and flies too.

-- Curtain call 2 --

Large pieces of heavy fabric, such as an old bedspread or throw, will often make the perfect door curtain for draughty areas of the house such as the front or back entrance.

-- Foiled again --

Aluminium foil is not just for keeping sandwiches fresh – it can help keep your fabrics crispy and sharp, too. Secure a sheet underneath the ironing board cover to stop the steam from penetrating the padding. The job is immediately made much faster and easier as steam is deflected back into the article being ironed.

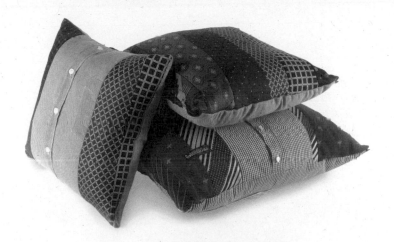

Design example
**Barley Massey
Remember Me**
Barley Massey has been
producing a range of interior
furnishings made from recycled
materials since the mid-
1990s, when she established
her Fabrications shop and
creative hub in London. Her
commissioning service,
Remember Me, tapped into
a popular niche – converting
clients' cherished textiles
(be they baby clothes, school
uniform, or an absent lover's
pyjamas) into cushions, pillows,
blankets and throws. Buttons
and fastenings are left on and
incorporated as "interactive
elements", which, says Massey,
provide greater connection
and comfort.

Design example
TING

TING was founded by London-based Inghua Ting in 2000, with a simple collection of cushions and seating handwoven from seatbelt fabric. With sustainability in mind over the fabric's novelty value, Ting saw in seatbelts a highly functional and durable material for luxury products. Later innovations also saw her exploiting the rigorously tested safety benefits of seatbelts with a range of luggage, storage containers and baskets.

Design example
Zoe Murphy
Margate collection
British designer Zoe Murphy
made a splash at her graduate
show with a range of furniture
and textile pieces inspired by her
seaside hometown of Margate.
Renovating, reworking and
generally upcycling mid-20th-
century furniture using prints,
engravings and new upholstery,
Murphy's colourful themed
collections were as sustainable
as they were popular. To make an
upholstery fabric for a vintage
stool, Murphy recycled and
dyed silk she had rescued from
old wedding dresses, before
handprinting it with images
of Margate.

-- Tight corner --

If you have lots of pairs of old tights, you can braid them together and use the resulting material to make poofs, rugs and other items. Cut old pairs of tights into strips and knot them together into a long length of about 12–15 m. Take three strips and braid them. Create a spiral with the braid, sewing each piece of the spiral to the next piece as it comes around. Like an express rag rug the result – depending on the quality of the raw material – makes a mat for a pet or a rug for the living room. To make a poof, coil the braid into a rounded shape, as if building a coil pot from clay.

-- Caffeine fix --

An effective and natural way of giving cotton and linen fabrics an overhaul is to dye them with tea or coffee for a vintage look. Using five or six tea bags to every gallon of water, let them steep until a very dark brown, then add the fabric. If using coffee, secure the grounds inside an old pair of tights or stockings. As different teas and coffees will give different shades, it might be worth experimenting on scraps first. To set the colour, fill a vat with enough fresh water to cover the fabric. For every gallon used, add half a cup of white vinegar. Soak the dyed fabric for about 15 minutes before rinsing clean. Finally, press the material dry with an iron.

-- Sleeve it be --

One of those items you probably didn't know you needed, once you have witnessed the organizational heaven that is a plastic bag dispenser you may well find it to be thoroughly indispensable. The basic form is a long fabric tube that can be hung on the wall. The top (where you put the bags) is open, while the bottom (where you pull the bags out) is elasticated. Easily homemade using scraps of fabric, the device could also be improvised using a sleeve from an unwanted garment.

Design example
Alyce Santoro
Sonic Fabric
Texas-based artist Alyce
Santoro started making noises
in environmental design circles
when she discovered a way
to make fabric from recycled
audiotape. Sonic Fabric is
remarkable in that it's not only
a durable and environmentally
friendly new textile (now
manufactured by Designtex) but
it's also playable. A medley of
recordings by Santoro (including
musicians on subway platforms,
conversations, and city streets)
can be heard by running the tape
head of a revamped Walkman
over the fabric's surface.

Design example
London Transport Museum Moquette

The alcohol ban on the London Underground was possibly a good idea, but those in the know can still sup a gin martini on a seat covered with classic public transport moquette fabrics should they ever feel that strange nostalgic urge. Reissued in a range of furniture and home accessories using the super-durable natural wool-based fabrics last used on London's buses and Underground in the 1930s and 1980s, the retro fabrics have been repurposed by the likes of Ella Doran, Suck UK and W2.

Design example
Lost & Found

London-based Lost & Found reworks antique flags and bunting into cushions. Larger naval and ceremonial flags become elegant throws and drapes. In a nod (or should that be a wave) to the fabric's military history, the designers often add extra military decoration and embroidered detail to the items, while care is taken to get the best out of each original, removing stains and mending tears before remaking.

Design example
Lucy Fergus
Re-silicone
Recycling rubber silicone into lighting, floor coverings and other home accessories, Lucy Fergus founded her company, Re-silicone, in 2007. The materials-based designer has long specialized in weaving industrial waste into new products, concentrating on keeping her work environmentally friendly as well as unique and stylish.

-- Fit fur a king --

Make a throne for your own miniature oligarch by adapting your redundant fur coat (fake or not) for a baby. Even if the coat has recently fed a family of moths, have it cleaned, look for any good bits that can still be salvaged, cut it down and line it if necessary, and start fashioning accessories: a luxurious blanket to line baby's cot is a good starting point, requiring minimal work. If there's any spare still left the nipper can have some furry booties and perhaps a hat to match. If you don't have a baby, your shih-tzu might appreciate it too.

-- Baa tending --

Similarly a sheepskin rug that has been trampled too often could potentially be salvaged to line a cot. Alternatively it might be cut down to line an underwear drawer or used to make a cushion. For the latter, use the sheepskin only on one side of the cushion and use another fabric (such as a thick satin or suede) for the back to give extra tactile contrast.

-- Wrinkly pickers --

To salvage the wool from a loved but deceased woolly sweater, unpick it at the seams and unravel the lengths carefully. The wool will be crinkly so wash the yarn in warm water, and let it drip-dry over a shower head or similar. When the yarn has dried flat you can wind it up into fresh balls and keep it ready to be used again.

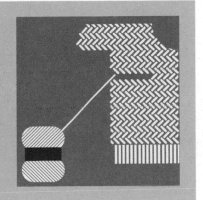

-- Care for the elderly --

If you have a collection of crockery that's extra special or extra old, a useful trick is to store the plates and saucers with a layer of scrap cotton between them to prevent scratches.

-- Scrambled pegs --

Make your own clothes-peg bag using a coathanger. Using any durable material (preferably waterproof if you're going to leave it outside on the line) cut a strip the same width as the hanger, and fold it over the crossbar to form a pocket. Sew the sides together, leaving the top open, and pop your pegs inside.

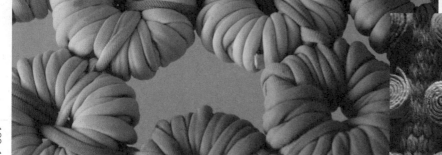

Design example
Claudia and Monica Araujo
Tecelagem Manual

Brazilian sisters Claudia and Monica Araujo established their textiles design company in 1992. After extensive research into weaving and frustrated with the limited threads available on the market in Brazil, the pair began innovating using unusual raw materials such as *rami*, a fibre usually used to tie coffee sacks, *piaçava*, a waste product from broom factories, and banana fibres. The Tapete Cabeludo is one of the company's most successful products, made using otherwise redundant scraps of polyamide from the textile industry. Another range, taPET, is handwoven from fibres made from recycled plastic bottles.

Design example
Greetje van Tiem
Indruk
Read all about it – today's news, according to Dutch designer Greetje van Tiem – is tomorrow's textiles. With a single page of a broadsheet she can spin twenty metres of yarn ready to be woven into all kinds of fabrics, from carpets to curtains and upholstery. The yarn retains its newspaper texture and appearance in its new incarnation. Although parts of the text remain visible, however, it's no longer possible to read the headlines, so you don't have to worry about your curtains becoming out of date.

-- Match making --

One way to tidy up mismatched dining chairs is to sew a set of ultra-simple slip covers for the backs. Measure the chair before you start and use newspaper to make a pattern that you can trace onto the fabrics. Finish it off with some ribbon ties at the bottom corners for a special homespun craft-queen look.

-- Tea's made --

You might not have bargained on how many solutions you'd find in this book for making a tea cosy, but it's important to be exhaustive in these matters. Should the leggings or sweater sleeves not do the trick, try searching around for an old woolly beanie hat – even better if it has a hole in it already (for the spout) and a pompom on top, of course. If not, just make the adjustments accordingly.

-- Egg warmers --

There's nothing on the breakfast table you can't keep cosy with an old and lonely legwarmer. And should your *Fame* days be long-gone, sleeves from an old woollen sweater will also do the job. Use them as tea cosies, mug cosies, coffee-pot cosies and porridge-bowl cosies. If you're blessed with a very little redundant sweater with very little sleeves you'll find it makes a rather fabulous egg cosy.

-- Plate-glass windows --

Liven up a set of glass plates with patterned fabric. Apply a thin layer of Mod Podge glue to the back of the plate and (quickly, as the glue dries fast) position the fabric over the top. Press the fabric to remove any air bubbles, then trim any excess fabric from around the edges of the plate. Let it dry before applying another thin layer of glue over the fabric. When the whole thing is thoroughly dry sand the glued side down until soft, add a layer of varnish (fabric-side only) and you're done. Bear in mind that the plate will no longer be dishwasher-safe, but it's a small sacrifice for a pretty pattern.

Design example
Kathrine Wardropper

Designer Katherine Wardropper builds three-dimensional textile pieces using coils of ribbon that she makes herself by cutting fabric into sheets. The intricate and distinctive results have won her many awards and prestigious commissions. Applied as wall art in high-end interiors or as decorative touches for mirrors, cushions, tables and chairs, Wardropper's works are all bespoke or limited-edition pieces, handcrafted by the designer herself in her London studio.

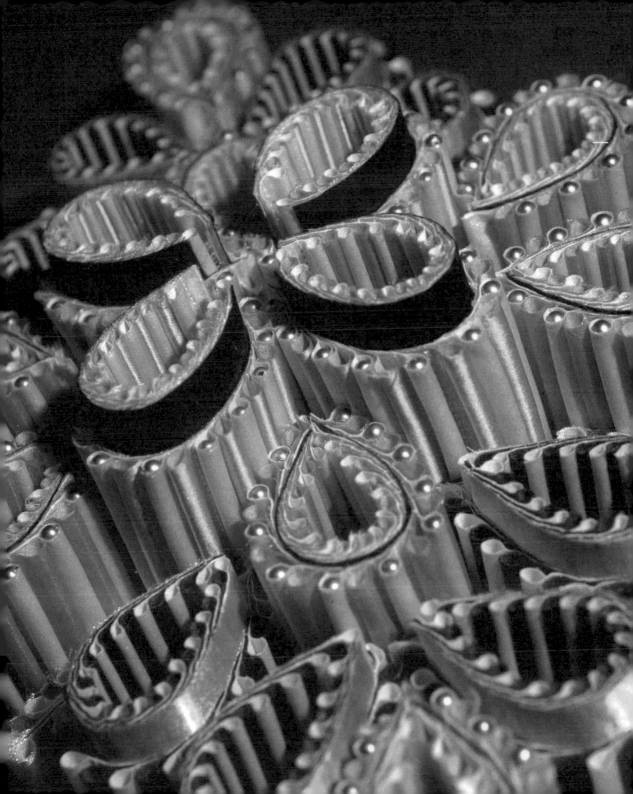

Design example
Abigail Brown

Londoner Abigail Brown is famous for her homemade soft creatures, which are designed and created to order using recycled fabrics and buttons. The line has evolved to include wall art, with Brown undertaking commissions for three-dimensional stuffed murals featuring birds and animals depicted in all kinds of magical settings.

-- Give us a P! --

One of the simplest and most instantly rewarding ways to reinvent a ball of wool is to make a pompom with it. For anyone who's forgotten how: cut two circles of card, about the same size that you want your finished pompom to be, and cut a round hole in the centre of each. Holding them together, wind a ball of yarn through the centre and around the outside until you've built up a thick layer of yarn, completely covering the two layers of card. Take some scissors and cut the yarn around the edge of the outside ring before taking a new piece of yarn and tying it securely between the two pieces of card, holding all the wool together in the centre. Remove the card and admire your fabulous creation.

-- Give us an O! --

Pompom applications are as multiple and varied as the poses of the bounciest cheerleader. The most traditional, of course, is to use a pompom to top off a tea cosy.

-- Give us an M! --

You could also get creative by using a pompom as a light-pull, or sewing little tiny ones around the edge of a tablecloth as a trimming. Christmas decorations are another popular application. You can also take extra-large pompoms and use them in place of cushions, or stitch together a bunch of small ones to make a little mat. Experiment using different types of twine for extra-fabulous pompompousness.

London-based Donna Wilson is often credited with the renaissance of knitting in fashionable circles. Generating a cult following for her subversive and adorable knitted monsters, Wilson quickly started winning commissions from furniture and upholstery manufacturers, going on to design and make knitted poofs and sofas for SCP, among other projects. Professing to love the fact that it is possible to construct a fabric out of a ball of yarn, Wilson has also always used fabric scraps in her work; indeed her monsters originated as an efficient ways to use up her odds and ends – but they quickly became her bestselling product.

Design example
Danielle Proud
Fun on the Floor
In a campaign to redefine the art of carpeting, interior designer and queen craft-pundit Danielle Proud took over a five-storey house in London's Camden and covered six contrasting themed rooms with traditional and contemporary carpet samples. The results were an inspiration to anyone who has kept old carpet tile samples under the stairs for want of something to do with them. Proud's ideas included a "patchwork carpet" on the stairs in the style of an American midwestern quilt, and a moose-head "carpet puzzle" on the walls.

-- Vegetable DIY 1 --

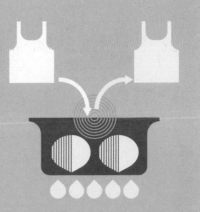

Boiling up onion skins will make a traditional all-natural dye for woollens and cotton. Although the shade will depend on what kind of onions you use, the general rule is that red-onion skins will result in a salmon-pink shade, and white-onion skins give a orangey yellowish hue. Next time you have a craving for an onion tart, keep the skins back after cooking and tear them into small pieces. Boil them in water for between 30 minutes and an hour, stirring regularly to get as much colour from them as possible. Strain the water and discard the skins. When the water has cooled add the material to be dyed and let it soak until it achieves the colour intensity you're after. Handwash in cool water and maybe add a few drops of peppermint essential oil to get rid of any lingering onion smell.

-- Vegetable DIY 2 --

Beetroot is famed for its ability to stain everything it touches a deep shade of pink. Harnessing this potent power as a dye involves little more than crushing the beetroot into salted water and boiling the fabric for a few hours until it reaches the desired colour. However, as beet juice is water-soluble, colourfastness can be a problem, and vinegar won't fix the dye. Your fabulous new fuschia frieze might knock the socks off your neighbour's tea-dyed tablecloth, but bear in mind that the more you wash beet-dyed fabric the paler it will become.

-- Tip-top tip 1 --
In case your mother never told you – remember to always mend tears, small holes and rips in any fabric before laundering it. The spin cycle just makes things worse.

-- Tip-top tip 2 --
If you need to mend a large hole, try reinforcing the area with net first to form a foundation for the stitches and to prevent the mend from puckering.

Design example
Elisabeth Nossen
Topi Stool

As the disposal of industrial textiles is illegal in Norway (from 2009) the surplus is generally given to charity and reused, while lower-quality fabrics are shredded into fine threads and used as insulation in buildings or as filling material in emergency blankets. Designer Elisabeth Nossen uses this shredded fabric material, which is called "shoddy", to replace the plastic foam in upholstered furniture. The Topi stool is a reupholstered secondhand foot stool Nossen purchased from a Salvation Army shop.

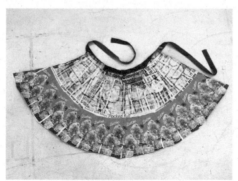

Design example
Emma Neuberg

As an artist and researcher specializing in recycling plastics and synthetics, Emma Neuberg is of the opinion that it's better to exploit a plastic bag's in-built longevity before consigning it to the recycling depot. One of Neuberg's ideas is to laminate the bags (or images cut from them) onto vintage denim – revamping the fabric with the plastic and making it waterproof at the same time.

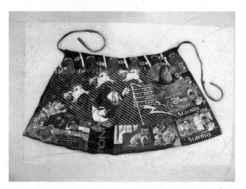

Design example
Andreas Linzner
Terrycloth Pets
Andreas Linzner found such a
successful niche in recycling
retro terrycloth towelling from
the 1950s, 60s and 70s into
adorable animals. Having studied
men's tailoring and textile art in
Nuremberg, Linzner fell in love
with the fabric after discovering
a number of flamboyant and
original towelling designs at a
flea market. He set up studio
in Hamburg and began selling
terrycloth elephants in 2001.

-- Duvet me fah so la teatowel --

Wartime rationing saw the most intriguing incarnations of all household linens. What started out as a duvet cover, for example, might go on to serve a useful life as a pair of curtains. Armed with a tape measure, a sewing machine and a bobbin of cotton or two, making drapes is something anyone can do in less than a day, and is a skill that can save you a good deal of money through not having to call in the professionals every time.

-- A --

When you move house it's unlikely that your old curtains will fit the new windows. Take them with you anyway, as they can usually be adjusted: curtains that are too large can easily be chopped down and re-hemmed, while those that are too short can often be lengthened by adding a trim.

-- B --

If the curtains really have outlived their time at the windows, they might be chopped down into smaller pieces of fabric and used to make other useful items. A laundry bag, for example, uses just two rectangular pieces sewn together along three sides. Or it might make a nice cushion cover or two, or a teatowel and perhaps a matching table runner...

-- C --

...Which in turn, when finally defunct as a centrepiece, can be doubled up, stitched along the sides and made into a peg-bag – which when it has outlived its usefulness, ultimately a dish-rag.

-- D --

The potential of an old duvet cover is limited only by your imagination. However, if whenever you do the drying up you're going to remember reading bedtime stories 20 years ago, let's hope you liked the pattern on that bedspread.

Design example
Seija Lukkala
Globe Hope
Seija Lukkala founded Globe Hope in 2002 with a mission to create textile products from materials such as old hospital textiles, army wear and industry offcuts, by recutting, resewing, redying and reprinting. Lukkala partnered with Anna Huoviala and went on to develop home accessories as well as a fashion brand. Military wear in particular is designed to be hard-wearing; repurposed as cushions, aprons and oven mitts, Globe Hope certainly puts it to the ultimate test.

STEP-BY-STEP

Sweater it out

There are many uses for old pillowcases – but when all you have is the shirt on your back, you have to start from scratch. An old T-shirt will easily make a serviceable covering for a pillow, while if you have two old sheets to spare, you can sew them up around three sides for a duvet cover. Leave one short side open for inserting and removing the duvet itself and add buttons or ribbons as fasteners. Meanwhile, sweaters that are past wearing can become cosy cushion covers in no time. To create pieces large enough to work with, use the body and sleeves patchworked together.

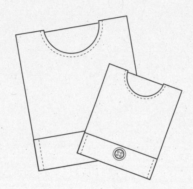

You will need:

_ Old long-sleeved sweaters or T-shirts
_ Sewing machine and thread
_ Scissors
_ Pins
_ Buttons or ribbons (for fastening)
_ Pillow or cushion

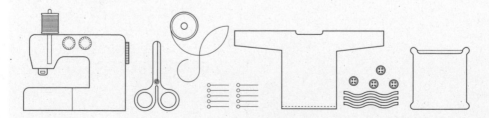

1_ Take the garment and turn it inside-out.

2a Pin up the sleeves in a straight line where they meet the body. Sew along the pins so that the side seams of the garment continue up to the shoulder. Close up the neckline in the same way – try to achieve as straight a line as possible – shoulder seam to shoulder seam. Your ability to do this will depend on the neck line of the original garment – if it's a boatneck, no problem, but if you're starting with a scoopneck or V-neck top, you can use scrap fabric from the sleeves to fill in the gap.

2b Trim off the excess fabric, and you should be left with a pocket – sides and top sewn closed, the bottom of the garment still open.

3_ Turn right-side out again and insert the cushion or pillow.

4 To hide the cushion (or pillow), take one of the sleeves you have just lopped off and cut and hem it to form a strip the same width as the opening of the cushion.

5_ Sew one edge of the strip to the inside of the opening to form a flap. Tuck the flap under the pillow.

6_ Add fastenings such as buttons or ribbons to keep the cover closed over the flap.

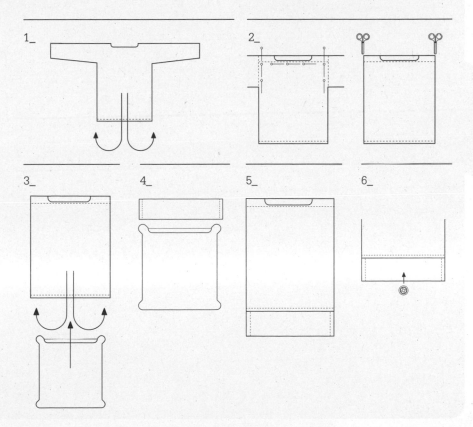

CLEANING, APPLIANCES & HOUSEHOLD MANAGEMENT

Refrigerators, kitchen utensils, cleaning

potions, ironing boards and rubber bands

-- High ho silver lining --

To banish the cold and loneliness after all the party guests have left, take that deflated helium balloon, cut it along the seams and stick it – shiny-side-out – to a board. Put the board behind a radiator to reflect the heat back into the room. It should also reduce the heating bills a little – which will help when saving up for the next festivities.

-- Forking out the extra --

Cutlery can prove to be as useful in the tool shed as it is in the dining room, so it's worth keeping a few old knives, forks, spoons and chopsticks to hand when DIYing as you can never know when you'll need them. Discarded table knives are good for applying polyfilla and grouting tiles, for example, while the back of a spoon will help you open a jammed up tin of paint.

-- Band of marigold --

If those trusty washing-up gloves are no longer watertight, worry not: they still have the potential to make very sturdy rubber bands. Cut across the glove in suitable widths for a splendid selection of good rubber bands of different sizes – most useful in any household.

-- Pining over you --

When stuffed with pinecones, cardboard toilet-paper rolls can also make wonderful kindling, emitting a homely woody aroma as they burn.

Design example
Pervisioni
Bottle Openers
Pervisioni's line of bottle openers
is created through modifying
selected knives, ranging from
pristine new name-brand
examples to factory rejects and
secondhand knives. An exercise
in functional reassignment, if
you will, the knives still retain
their histories and something
of their original purpose.

Design example
Od-do Arhitekti
Spoon Scissors
With a few strategic cuts, a
hinge and a knife sharpener,
Belgrade design consultancy
Od-do fabricated these home-
made scissors from a pair of
old spoons.

Design example
Heineken
WOBO (World Bottle)
In 1963, Alfred Heineken had a brilliant idea. On a recent visit to the Caribbean he had seen hundreds of bottles littering the beaches. Noticing that another of the islands' biggest problems was a serious lack of affordable building supplies, he put two and two together and came up with the beer brick. With Dutch architect John Habraken, Heineken designed a glass bottle with a shape that gave it a built-in second life as a building block.

-- Lemon aid --

Lemon juice is natural super-cleaner that dissolves soap scum and hard water deposits and gives brass and copper a nice shine. Mix it with baking soda to make a paste that will clean almost anything. If you're in a hurry, just cut a lemon in half and sprinkle baking soda on the cut section to scrub dishes, surfaces and stains.

-- A saucy top --

For a professional and personal finish to a birthday cake decorate it with icing script. Instead of writing with fiddly icing bags – a nightmare to control and unsatisfying to lick clean afterwards – use an empty ketchup or mustard bottle. Just make sure it is clean and fill it with your icing mixture; flip off the lid and scribble away. The rest of the icing in the bottle can be saved conveniently in the refrigerator for the next bake-off.

-- Pump stake --

Cut up an old sponge to form a neat collar around the neck of a pump-action soap bottle. The collar makes it harder to dispense more soap than is needed each time.

-- Static spacetime --

Tumble-dryer sheets are specifically designed to help eliminate static cling, so it follows that a quick wipe with a used sheet will keep dust from resettling on a television or computer screen. Sheets are also especially effective in collecting pet hairs, dust and sawdust. An old housewives' trick is to use them when sewing to prevent the thread from tangling: rub the needle with the dryer sheet first. The sheets even help in washing dishes. Let a dryer sheet soak in a pan with water overnight, and the anti-static agent will loosen cooked-on food.

-- Dressing down --

Save the balsamic for the salads, but mildly acidic white vinegar dissolves dirt and hard-water deposits. Diluted with water (one part vinegar to one part water) it makes a good solution for cleaning hardwood floors. Vinegar is a natural deodorizer, absorbing odours instead of covering them up, and the smell evaporates as it dries, so you don't need to worry that your bathroom will smell like a chip shop when you've finished. Vinegar also cuts detergent residue, so it works as an ideal fabric-softener substitute for those with sensitive skin. Mix a solution in a spray bottle and keep it on hand for countertops and floors. Undiluted, it will tackle tougher tasks like the toilet and hard water deposits on shower heads.

-- Bottled up --

It is worth keeping any attractive glass bottles you find; you can decant detergents and liquid soaps into them. An old Victorian bottle dug up from the garden is ideal, but even an old glass ketchup bottle can look attractive beside the kitchen sink. Fit the bottle with a pourer or a cork and dilute the product as necessary. Often detergents are made much stronger than they need to be in order to get the job done, and households with a soft water supply generally need to use less product than those with hard water.

-- Bubble and squeak --

The citric acid in Alka-Seltzer, together with its remarkable effervescent action, makes it an excellent lavatory cleaner. Drop a few tablets in to the bowl and leave them for about half an hour, after which a few passes with a toilet brush will restore your throne to its former radiance.

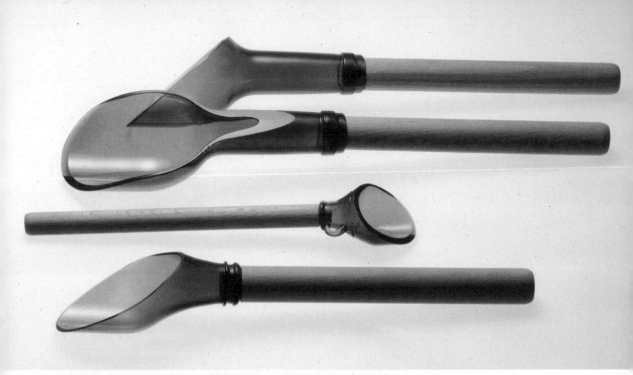

Design example

Laurence Brabant
Cold Cuts

Glass artist Laurence Brabant is based in Paris, where she graduated from the École Supérieure des Arts Appliqués Duperré in 1997. Rapidly snapped up by the FNAC (Fond National d'Art Contemporain) her stunning tableware designs have inspired collaborations with the Venetian glass manufacturer Salviati, fashion designers Martin Margiela and Jean-Paul Gaultier, Philippe Starck and glamorous florist Christian Tortu. Although usually creating her pieces from scratch, Cold Cuts is a series of scoops and spoons elegantly cut from wine bottles.

STEP-BY-STEP

Freeze!

Many people use this technique of freezerless freezing to make instant homemade ice cream, but it's also a very efficient method of chilling wine or mineral water in a matter of minutes (be careful not to freeze the wine – it works more quickly than you'd expect). Although water normally freezes at 0 degrees C (32 degrees F), when it comes into contact with salt it stays liquid at much lower temperatures, making a solution that is cold enough to freeze other substances. To maximize your remaking score, use old zip-loc bags that are on their last legs for the two outer layers.

You will need:

- _ 4 cups of crushed ice
- _ 4 tablespoons of salt
- _ 2 quart-sized zip-loc bags
- _ 1 gallon-sized zip-loc freezer bag
- _ Gloves

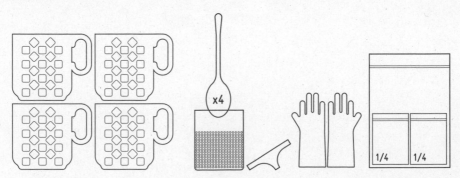

1_ If you are chilling something in a
   precooled container, such as a bottle
   of wine, skip to Step 3. Otherwise,
   place (or pour) the substance to be
   frozen inside one of the smaller bags
   and seal tightly, squeezing out as
   much air as possible.

2_ Put the smaller bag inside the other
   quart-sized bag, and seal tightly,
   squeezing out the air. (The second
   bag minimizes the risk of salt and
   ice getting mixed up with the food.)

3_ Put the package inside the large bag
   and fill the space around it with ice.

4_ Sprinkle the salt on top of the ice, seal
   the large bag and put your gloves on.

6_ Shake the bag, moving the ice around
   to ensure it surrounds the object
   completely and the salt is distributed
   evenly. Depending on the item it
   ought to be frozen in around five
   to eight minutes (or less, if you're
   chilling wine).

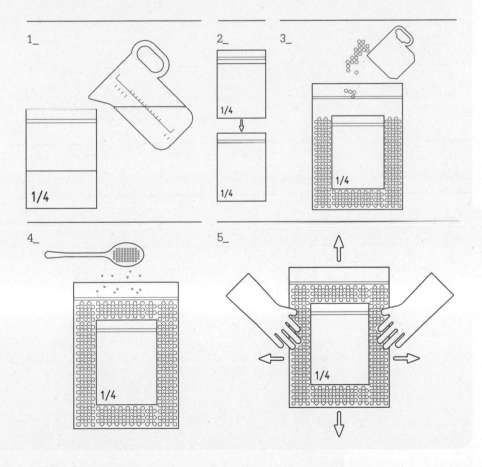

-- Hose there --

A leaky garden hose isn't completely redundant: it has many qualities in common with that favourite reusable: the bicycle inner tube, the reincarnations of which know no bounds. Sections of a hose also make perfect grips for garden tools. Slit the hose along its length and slip it over the handle of your trowel or bucket. Garden hose can also be used around the chains of a swing to protect little fingers.

-- Homemade T-bags --

For a reusable shopping bag, there's nothing easier than simply taking an old vest – the bigger the better – and sewing up the bottom. T-shirts can be adapted in the same way: just lop off the sleeves and cut a deep neckline before you sew up the bottom.

-- Wiper club 1 --

A windscreen wiper that doesn't wipe the windscreen anymore might not be completely defunct. Detach the arm and add a handle to make a squeegee for washing windows and countertops at home.

-- Wiper club 2 --

Remove the rubber from the windscreen wiper and affix it to the bottom of an upright shower door to act as a gasket and water seal (you may need rubber from two wipers to make it long enough).

-- Lettuce pray --

Forget the double-barrelled plastic tubs that call themselves salad spinners. Take an old dry dishcloth, place the wet leaves in the centre, gather up the ends and hold securely. Head outside and swing it around vigorously like you're an Olympic hammer-thrower – but don't let go.

-- Take the plunge --

What use is a cafetière plunger without the rest of the coffee pot?
Depending on the model you have, if you remove the gauze layer
it can make a surprisingly effective potato masher. It is also possible
to dismantle the plunger into its component parts to make a portable
masher, which is useful if you don't care for instant potato flakes from
a box while camping. Who could ask for more?

-- Jug or nought --

What use is a cafetière coffee pot without its plunger? Why, it's the
perfect jug for hot milk, gravy or other sauces.

-- Eggs for tea --

When stove-top vessels are in short supply, remember
that not only can tea water be boiled in a saucepan,
but eggs can also be cooked in the teakettle. Just make
sure to give the kettle a good wash afterward to get rid
of the egg taste. Although there's nothing to stop you
from trying, boiling eggs in electric kettles is like playing
Russian roulette, staking all your future cups of tea on the
provision that the egg won't break while boiling and ruin
the heating element.

-- Funnelly enough --

A wide plastic bottle with a comparatively
narrow neck can be adapted into a funnel by
cutting off the bottom half and removing the
cap. If your funnel is intended for dispensing
food, use a plastic bottle that has previously
held something edible or drinkable (avoid
bottles from toxic substances such as
cleaning products or solvents).

Design example
**Nicolas Le Moigne
Watering Can**
Trained at the prestigious École
Cantonale d'Art Lausanne
(ECAL), Swiss product designer
Nicolas Le Moigne had several
of his designs in production even
before he graduated. One of
them, for Italian design company
Viceversa, was the Watering Can:
a plastic handle and spout that
can be screwed onto an empty
water bottle.

Design example
Kyouei
Umbrella Pot
In this ceramic umbrella
stand by Japanese designers
Kyouei,a common domestic
inconvenience has been
poetically reconsidered. Instead
of forming dank puddles in the
hallway, the drips of rainwater
from a soggy brolly become a
life-sustaining resource for a
small plant.

-- Gone with the wind --

A fan that has rusty blades needn't be chucked if the motor still works. Simply make your own "blades" using scrap fabric. When the fan is turned on the fluttering fabric will still keep you cool.

-- Nice rack --

Metal pull-out racks from an unwanted oven – scrubbed and shiny – will quite often transfer happily to the bathroom where, mounted vertically on a wall, they can be used to hang washcloths and towels.

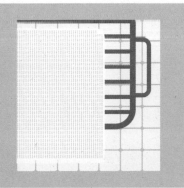

-- Rising scale --

Fishy heaven probably doesn't have fish tanks – just vast sparkling lagoons where your departed scaly friends can frolic for all eternity while you figure out what to do with the ten-gallon glass box they've left behind. If you're tired of keeping fish or simply too sentimental to think about replacing poor Guppy, you have a number of options here: acquire some terrapins, or grow some herbs.

-- Plug on at it --

Bath plug disappeared without a trace? You're not alone – it's a problem more common than logic would dictate that it should be. Luckily an old rubber shoe-sole can do the job instead. Cut it down carefully to size, affix a string or chain (a loop nail or screw should hold these in place) and you're back in bathtime business.

-- Totally degrading --

As they are entirely biodegradable, shredded phone book pages make good mulch to keep weeds down in the garden.

-- Waft living --

A scented dryer sheet can be used as an air freshener almost anywhere you can imagine. Place an individual sheet in a drawer; hang one in the closet, in your locker at the gym or under the seat of your car. A sheet can prevent musty smells from building up when placed inside books, luggage and storage boxes that you know will not see much use. For the sweaty soled, it's not a bad idea to put a sheet into a pair of shoes or trainers to help deodorize them overnight.

-- Oomph a loofah --

An old loofah can be cleaned by soaking it in vinegar (white or apple cider vinegar work best), after which it can either be returned to bathing service or used to wash the dishes. If the vinegar doesn't get the loofah as clean as you'd like, boil it afterwards, and it should come out clean as new.

-- Put a sock in it --

Beat the elves in the washing machine who always manage to steal one sock. Keep the lone remaining socks in a box, washed and ready to be used for dusting. Better than conventional dusters in lots of ways, they can be used glove-style to give super-accurate cleaning power when cleaning fiddly spots between stair-rails and around chair legs.

-- Pinnies and needles --

If the pattern is pretty enough to save, it's easy to adapt an old pillowcase to make an apron. Simply cut or fold up the open end and stitch along the sides to instantly make two deep pockets at the front. Then add a ribbon at the top to tie around the waist.

-- Feeling flush --

Toilets are invariably are made with tanks far larger than necessary to flush effectively. An old water-saving trick is to dam the tank. Fill an old container with sand, stones and water – a plastic bottle or a glass jar is perfect – and place it into the tank. The size of the container dictates the amount of water that will be saved at every flush.

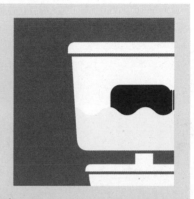

-- Set and match --

What do you do with old tennis balls when their rallying days are over? Give them to the dog. But what if you don't have a dog? No problem: an old tennis ball can become a useful household implement. Cut a small X on its surface and attach a broom handle to make an instant tool with which to remove black rubber skid marks from wooden floors.

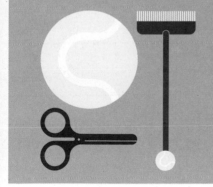

-- Cut some rug --

Shaving cream can be used to clean up spills and stains on carpets or rugs. After wetting the spot thoroughly, apply the foam, leave for a few seconds and then dab it off with a clean towel or sponge. Check for colourfastness by applying a small test patch to a discreet area of the rug before you begin.

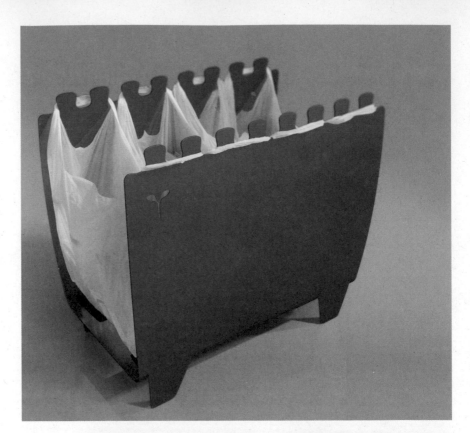

Design example

Sprout Design
Binvention

One of the aims of London-based Sprout Design is to add value to raw materials, which is admirably demonstrated in the company's first self-initiated product, the Binvention. An instant hit when it was launched in 2006, the Binvention is a simple and compact frame structure that holds four plastic carrier bags, allowing users to compartmentalize their rubbish for recycling.

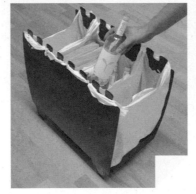

-- Fashion revival --

Bring an old piece of furniture back to life using a home-made "reviver" mixture: one part raw linseed oil to nine parts white spirit. After cleaning the item with soapy water and drying, shake the reviver mixture thoroughly and apply with cotton wool. Any leftovers can be stored in a cool place in a clearly labeled and tightly sealed bottle.

-- Adventures in ice-making --

An old fridge egg rack with moulded recesses can be used in place of an ice-cube tray in an emergency. Other candidates for this repurpose include silicon baking moulds (especially those intended for cupcakes), jelly moulds, balloons (long, thin ones are best) and saucepans. If using the latter, simply heat the saucepan a little when you take it out of the freezer to release the block of ice. For crushed ice, put the larger resulting ice "sculptures" in a plastic bag, and smash them on a chopping board with a rolling pin.

-- Pump stakes --

Save any old pump-action bottles, wash them out and refill them with homemade salad dressing and sauces. Where the bottles originally contained detergents or toiletries it is wisest to reuse them in the same context, perhaps for homemade cleaning solutions, to avoid contaminating your ketchup.

-- Do or dial --

Old phone books can make excellent fire starters for a wood-burning fireplace or outdoor fire pit. Balled-up or shredded phone book pages also make an effective packaging filler, a happy alternative to those polystyrene peanuts that make some people (especially environmentalists) cringe.

Design example
Peter van der Jagt
Bottoms-Up Doorbell

Announcing guests with a welcoming clink of wine glasses, Peter van der Jagt's doorbell for Droog has become a design classic since it was launched in 1994. Granted, there's not a lot of competition when it comes to iconic doorbells, but Bottoms-Up isn't just a quirky conversation piece; it's a serious rethinking of an ordinary product. Van der Jadt was keen to make the workings of the doorbell transparent and succeeded most literally.

-- Coaster coast --
Old CDs, which are heat-proof, make useful coasters for hot drinks.
Keep one to hand in the home office, where it will look contextually
appropriate while supporting your perpetual mug of tea.

-- Getting tipsy --
Two wine corks – especially the plastic ones – strategically placed
(lengthways so they won't roll) under each back corner of a laptop
will incline it to a more comfortable typing angle.

-- Old flames --
For robust fire starters fill up each cup of an old egg box with dryer
lint. Melt some old candle stubs and pour over the lint to seal. It's a
three-in-one recycling extravaganza, and it will get a wood or charcoal
fire started easily without the danger or smell of lighter fluid.

-- Toasted flatbread --

If you find yourself with a spare working iron, then
consider relocating it to the kitchen, where it can
be put to work making fabulous toasted sandwiches
and panini.

-- Clean break 1 --
Modern bagless vacuum cleaners often come with the added benefit
of removable dust collectors, which – when the rest of the machine
bites the dust (or rather doesn't, anymore) – can start a new life as
a jug, watering can, or kitchen-counter scrap bin.

-- Clean break 2 --
Another useful vacuum-cleaner organ that can easily be repurposed is
the hose. Split the tube down the middle and cut it into short lengths
that can be used as cable tidies to keep cords and wires from tangling.

STEP-BY-STEP

Chillin' room

In many developing countries, fridges and freezers are not only expensive and hard to come by; they're also pretty useless in communities without electricity. Long-term storage of food therefore requires a more inventive solution.

Using an idea revived recently by Muhammed Bah Abba, a Nigerian teacher, farmers in warm climates now often build homemade pot-in-a-pot fridges, originally known as zeer pots, using basic clay or terra-cotta vessels, sand and water. Bah Abba, who came from a family of potters, became famous after receiving the $75,000 Rolex Award for Enterprise for his cooling system, which brought major improvements to the lives of many Nigerians. Eggplants, for example, last for 27 days rather than 3, while tomatoes and peppers stay fresh for weeks.

The design is as simple as it is effective. One pot is placed inside the other, and damp sand is packed in the space between them. Keeping the sand constantly moist enables evaporation to cool the produce kept inside the inner pot, making it last much longer in a hot climate.

You will need:

_ Two large clay or terra-cotta pots. One pot must be smaller than the other pot. Check that the smaller pot fits inside the larger one with 1–3 cm of space around it.

_ If there are holes in the pots, you'll need something to plug these: for example, clay, large pebbles or cork.
_ Water
_ Sand
_ Cloth or towel for covering

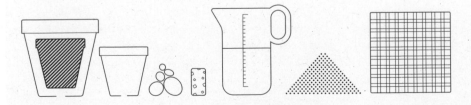

1_ Fill in any holes at the base of the pots to prevent water escaping or leaking on to the food.

2_ Fill the base of the larger pot with enough sand so that the rims of the two pots are at the same height when the smaller pot is placed inside. Then fill all around the small pot with sand, right to the top.

3_ Pour as much water into the sand as you can, until it is completely soaked. Take a cloth or towel and dip it into water. Place it over the top of the inner pot so that it covers it completely.

4_ The inner pot will start cool down, and *voilà* – you have a new fridge.

5_ Keep the pots in a dry, ventilated space where the water can evaporate effectively, and the fridge won't be raided by hungry animals.

6_ The water will probably need to be topped up twice a day.

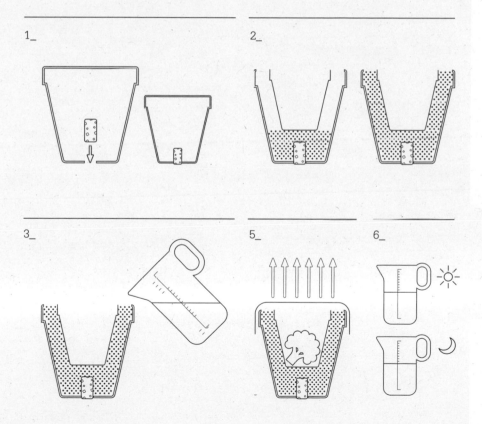

1_

2_

3_

5_

6_

-- Caffeine fix --

If you find yourself craving filter coffee but don't have proper coffee filters to hand, then you're in a bit of a fix. Never fear: kitchen roll, a clean tea towel or a scrap of muslin or gauze these will work almost as well. Mix the coffee and hot water in a jug, put the fabric or tea towel across a funnel and pour through the filter.

-- In the name of loaf --

Bread wrapped in a plastic grocery bag inside the bread bin will stay fresher for longer, as the safety holes in the bag allow it to breathe without going stale.

-- Foul play --

If you live next door to a golf course, and happen to keep your own chickens, you're in an ideal situation – you can use the stray golf balls as fake eggs to encourage your hens to start laying or to accept a new nesting box.

-- Down scale --

Particularly resourceful chefs might attach a beer-bottle top to a lollipop stick – spiky side out – to use as an ad hoc appliance for descaling fish on camping expeditions or at barbecues.

-- Grate expectations --

Metal cheese graters are usually consigned to the rubbish because they've gone rusty. Dispatch your old grater to the tool shed instead: they make useful rasps or chamfer planes for woodworking.

-- Leg'n chips --

An old pair of tights or stockings can be handy as an alternative to coffee filters or cheesecloth when straining frying oil in the kitchen so that it can be used again. With the oil in a jar, stretch the fabric over the top and secure it with an elastic band before pouring it through.

-- Yolk music --

For families who consume a great deal of eggs, the boxes can be used to sound-proof rooms in the house where building work is going on – the garage or perhaps even a teenager's bedroom. The shape makes them especially good at absorbing sound.

-- Wok's on next? --

Repurpose an old metal satellite dish as a barbecue pan, wok or paella dish. Make sure it's thoroughly clean and remove all wires and electronic components; then just add fire, oil and chicken legs.

-- Clean as a bristle --

Originally designed for cleaning hard-to-reach crevices, an old toothbrush can serve the same purpose around the house long after you've upgraded your dental hygiene equipment. Keep one or two old toothbrushes for scrubbing around drains and behind bathroom fixtures. They are also great for washing fiddly items such as ornaments and jewelry, or degreasing bicycle chains and car parts.

Design example
Sante Kim
Wine Bottle Speakers
In a sound solution that puts
the acoustic qualities of glass
to good use, Korean designer
Sante Kim recycled wine bottles
into flower-shaped speakers
that, with their highly sculptural
qualities, might be displayed
on a sideboard or hung from
the ceiling.

-- Aerial views --

With the advent of digital TV, those spiky analogue aerials are not long for this world. But across the globe, people are saying 'no' to the premature demise of these long-serving iconic objects of the 20th century, repurposing them for a new generation as mug trees, hand-towel racks, and budgie stands.

-- The trough gets going --

Refrigerators are notoriously difficult to dispose or recycle. But so long as there's a fashion for retro kitchenware, even relatively grotty examples can find a useful new life. An attractive model needs only a good clean before being moved into the sitting room to serve as a drinks cabinet. To make a sturdy and waterproof trunk for use in a shed or utility room, remove the shelving and lay the fridge on its back, or remove the door as well for an outdoor water trough.

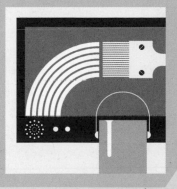

-- Flat liners --

You were so proud of that flat-screen TV once, but times change, and now you have a better one. Keep it in service by painting the screen with blackboard paint to make a novelty chalkboard.

-- Plate class --

With the simple acquisition of a grease pencil or water-based marker pen, any plain or light-coloured crockery instantly becomes a reusable memo pad. Attach the pencil with a length of string to a large plate so its use is immediately clear and the pencil won't go walkabout when you need to leave messages for family members. As it is also waterproof, the plate message board is ideal for outdoor use – perfect as a means to communicate with delivery people and the postman.

-- The way it rolls --

Making pizza, or pie, or pizza pie is nigh-on impossible if you don't own a rolling pin. An olive-oil bottle or any tall, slim glass bottle filled with water will do the job nicely. Be careful when you use it not to apply pressure to the fragile neck of the bottle, which can break. An extra tip is to chill the bottle in the fridge before rolling out pie crust or other cold-loving pastry doughs.

-- Raw magnetism --

Stereo speakers and electric motors in many household appliances contain strong magnets that can be extracted and reused in numerous applications, including a wall-mounted knife rack or a notice board.

-- Spit and polish --

Toothpaste can be used to clean much more than molars. Its very fine abrasive nature can help polish and clean the bottom of a cool iron, buff up the bathroom or kitchen chrome and clean stains off sinks. It also works to remove coffee and tea stains from the inside of mugs.

-- Ta-ta to tar --

Use a bit of WD-40 to get rid of tough black scuff marks or tar on a hard floor. Spray it on the marks lightly and it will make the stains much easier to scrub off. The oil-based solution shouldn't harm the surface of the floor.

Design example

Dmitry Zagga
Cup Speakers

Allegedly conceived when Latvian designer Dmitry Zagga found his credit card declined at the Apple Store, these iPod speakers, constructed from four paper cups and two toothpicks, were an instant hit across the blogosphere. Working on the same principle as the string-and-cup short-distance telephone that many people might remember from their childhoods, the amplification might not quite be to super-woofer standards, but it's better than nothing when a miniature party is required at short notice. To make the speakers, punch holes in the bottoms of two of the cups, position them on top of the other two, linking them together with the two toothpicks. Thread your earphones through the holes, and get down and boogie.

-- Where there's life, there's soap --

A quirky but age-old alternative to soap-on-a-rope, an old pair of tights can be put to good use in the bath or shower. Put soap in the end of each leg and hang up the tights, or cut one leg down to soap size and knot it. The soap will stay put, it won't leave grime on the side of the bath and it will last longer. The feet of the tights can also be filled with bath salts or herbs and used like a giant bath tea bag for a more aromatic cleansing experience.

-- Soap spuds --

A little trick to stop the bathroom mirror from steaming up is to take a small dollop of shaving foam and smear it onto the glass before a shower or bath. A longer-lasting but less well-known solution is to use a raw potato. After cleaning the mirror in the usual way, cut a potato in half and wipe the cut surface over the glass before wiping any residue away with a clean tissue.

-- Dental surgery --

Strangely, toothpaste is well known for repairing scratched CDs. If after more orthodox cleansing with a light detergent (no sponge) the CD keeps skipping, polish it with toothpaste using a cotton swab, rubbing gently over the scratches until they disappear. Wash the CD in water and dry it again – it ought to be good as new.

-- Soda commercial --

Baking soda has a mild abrasive action and natural deodorizing properties that make it a powerful replacement for commercial scouring powders and detergents. Sprinkle it onto a damp sponge to tackle grimy bathtub rings, or make a paste of baking soda and water, apply it to the tub or sink and leave it to stand for 10 or 20 minutes to soften caked-on dirt.

Raise a glass --

Rubbing (isopropyl) alcohol works with one part water and a little white vinegar to make an evaporating cleaner for glass and chrome fixtures.

-- What's the gloss? --

Most commercial furniture polish contains silicone oil, which can penetrate tiny cracks in the furniture finish and enter the wood – often causing problems whenever refinishing might be needed. Create a homemade version using lemon juice (to dissolve dirt and smudges) and olive oil (to shine and protect the wood). Use two parts oil to one part lemon juice to keep furniture surfaces clean and shiny enough to eat off. Or just to lick every now and then.

-- Overcome with emulsion --

When painting a room, line the paint tray with an old plastic bag before pouring in the paint. Cleaning up was never so easy.

-- Peel for help --

Freshen up a kitchen drain by running a whole lemon rind through the garbage disposal. Oranges and limes also work well.

-- Dish dude 1 --

Dishwashers are almost as fun as washing machines when they've reached the end of their serviceable lives. Dissect your old dishwasher into its constituent parts: the drawers and cutlery holder will usually work very effectively as draining racks beside the sink.

-- Dish dude 2 --

If washing up is really not your thing, or you already have a perfectly good draining rack, the drawers of a defunct dishwasher might find themselves reincarnated as desk trays. The plate dividers separate files, brochures and papers wonderfully. Use the cutlery rack as a pen tidy and give your whole desk a shiny-clean theme. It might not wash at the office, true, but if you work from home you can well afford to take office equipment snobbery with a pinch of (dishwasher) salt.

-- Bin dreaming --

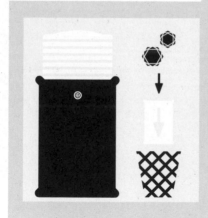

Pillowcases make very efficient liners for wicker wastebaskets. Especially useful for bedrooms where little nail clippings and hair from a hairbrush tend to slip through the weave of an unlined bin. An old cotton pillowcase is much more attractive than a plastic grocery bag (another traditional liner) and can be washed whenever the bins are changed.

-- Mop it --

Instead of spending all your hard-earned pennies on flash plastic mops of every variety, adapt your own for different tasks. For a dry mop that picks up dust, flour and animal hair before washing floors and other surfaces, wrap a worn-out soft flannel sheet or shirt around the bottom of your broom and dust away.

Design example
Gijs Bakker
Dishmop
Conceived by Gijs Bakker for
Droog Design in 2004, this stylish
reinvention of the ubiquitous
dishmop consists of a coloured
foam ball clamped between the
arms of a pair of steel tongs. For
those who don't want to splash
out on washing the crockery, a
similar result might be achieved
with a pair of salad servers and
a sponge.

STEP-BY-STEP

Don't cry over spilt milk

Whether you're up the creek without a paddle, or confronted with a spillage on a hard floor without a mop, it's time to get resourceful. While snapping a plank off the side of your boat might help in the first instance, a little more care and attention is required to make a sturdy and serviceable mop. The result is not only likely to last you longer than its shop-bought plastic equivalent, but the superior absorption of the old bath towels used for the mop head will soak up almost anything you throw at it.

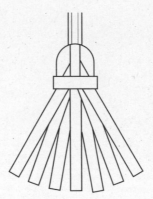

You will need:

_ Old bath towel
_ Scissors
_ Cable ties
_ Wooden broomstick

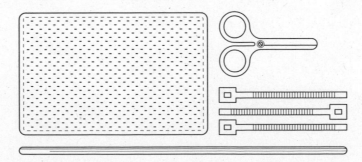

1_ Remove the hems from the towel and divide into strips. (A standard bath towel will make about twenty strips.)

2_ Keeping one strip back to use at the end, lay out the rest so that each slightly overlaps the next.

3_ Place the end of the stick on top of the overlapping strips so that the end of the stick is about 2 cm from the bottom edge of the strips. Roll together and secure tightly with a cable tie about 2 cm from the bottom edge of the stick.

4_ Once secured, turn the mop over so that the strips are hanging down. Use another cable tie to secure the towels in this direction.

5_ Snip off the end of the cable tie. For an optional touch of class, cover the cable tie by knotting the spare strip of towel over it.

1_

2_

3_

4_

5_

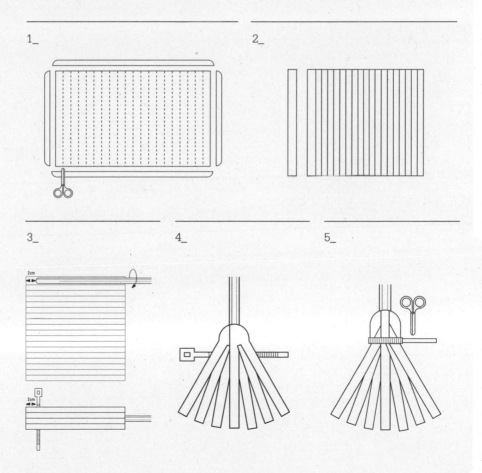

-- Daily grind --

If you've recently used a mortar and pestle, food processor or spice mill to grind strong spices, the flavour can be hard to wash off. Run a handful of uncooked rice through the appliance – any residue will disappear and prevent it from tainting your next recipe.

-- Potted plants --

Any number of old kitchen pots and pans can be strung up and reused as a hanging basket for herbs and flowers. Old colanders in particular are indispensable for their inbuilt drainage function.

-- Roll on home --

Cardboard tubes and toilet-paper rolls can be reused in hundreds of different ways. Tidy up a jungle of power leads by folding each cable back and forth a few times and pushing all the loops through the tube.

-- Pulp fiction --

Use a hand-powered kitchen whisk as an alternative paper shredder for old bank statements and credit card receipts. Fill a bucket half full with water and add the paper to be mulched. Leave for a couple of minutes until thoroughly soggy, and whisk away. The paper pulp can then be used to make homemade paper, moulded into new objects or thrown away securely.

-- Fur get it --

Old stockings and tights can be used to pick up animal hair from clothes and furniture; when rubbed they become charged with static electricity, which makes hair stick to them.

Design example
Tom Ballhatchet
Hamster Shredder
British designer Tom
Ballhatchet's unique contraption
combines a paper shredder
with a hamster cage. When the
hamster runs on his wheel, a
gear mechanism transmits the
power to the paper shredder,
turning unwanted documents
into his bedding. "For me, it
comments on the idea of all of
us being responsible for the
effect we are having on the
planet, as well as nodding
towards micro-generation as
a future source of power," says
the designer.

Design example
Zo-Loft
Din-ink
Pen caps tend to get their fair share of absent-minded chewing at the best of times, so a simple adaptation to make them into functional cutlery was a logical move. Perfect for dining 'al desko' the Din-ink range was designed by Italian company Zo-Loft to be entirely biodegradable, non-toxic and hygienic.

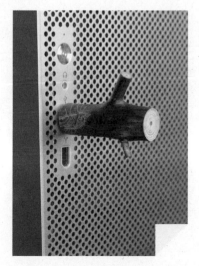

Design example
Studio OOOMS
Twig Memory Stick
Run by designers Guido
Ooms and Karin van Lieshout
in the Netherlands, Studio
OOOMS emphasizes striking
reinterpretations of everyday
items in its work. One idea that
captured the imagination of
the mass market was the Twig
memory stick. The sticks are
individually selected by
OOOMS and fixed to USB
memory sticks by hand.

-- Sud off --

When all things luxe were heavily rationed during the Second World War, nothing would be thrown away. When a bar of old soap was too small to use, the ends would be saved in a pot or jam-jar by the sink. When enough ends had been collected they could be melted down (as you would chocolate, in a glass bowl over boiling water) and remoulded into new bars.

-- Beer faced --

A makeshift bottle opener can be easily crafted using a small piece of wood and two screws. Fix the screws in the wood about 2 cm apart so that one will clamp the neck of the bottle while the other levers open the cap.

-- Whisky business --

Need a bit more oomph to your wrist action when it comes to whipping cream? Fix that old hand whisk securely to the bit of an electric drill and see the proof of the pudding in no time. (Try the lowest speed first to make sure you don't wind up with butter in the bowl – or cream on the ceiling.)

-- Totally tacky --

WD-40 can be used to clean dried glue off hard surfaces. Spray it onto the spot, wait for half a minute and wipe it all clean with a damp cloth. This is also an effective way to remove stickers from glass – the solvents in WD-40 cause the adhesive to lose its stickiness.

-- Pump some iron --

Remove a grease mark from wallpaper by ironing it – an old trick from pre-war days when lots of family homes had papered kitchens. Heat up the iron and unplug it. Cover the spot with a clean scrap of cotton and press the iron over the wall. Don't try this trick on vinyl wallpaper: it will melt.

-- Patent pending --

Some people consider a dairy-free diet good for the gut, but their handbags and shoes might not be as clean and shiny as those belonging to their cream-loving cousins. Milk, you see, is a perfect polish for patent leather. Dab on, buff off, and admire your reflection in the results.

-- Beta pan --

Use a utility or craft knife to cut down a large plastic detergent bottle to fashion a makeshift dustpan. Keep the section with the handle intact if you can, but make sure to leave a flat edge wide enough to gather up the dust. If you're short of a broom, an old paintbrush will do the trick nicely.

-- Wood you believe it --

Make water stains (such as rings from glasses) on a wooden table disappear by using a magical mixture of salt and water. Mix the salt with a few drops of water to form a paste, and gently rub it onto the ring with a soft cloth or sponge. Work the mixture into the wood until the mark is gone, and then restore your table to its shiny old self with a good furniture polish.

Design example
Creative Paper Wales
Sheep Poo Paper Air Freshener
Sheep droppings are not the most obvious ingredients for an air freshener, but Creative Paper Wales wanted to make a point. The company's handcrafted papers and paper products are as clean and hygienic as any. The company can make paper from practically any material containing good cellulose fibres (such as rag and textile off-cuts), but as most sheep only digest half of the cellulose they eat, it is especially well suited to the cause. After the sheep poo is collected, it is sterilized by boiling, and washed repeatedly over several days until it has lost approximately half its original weight, leaving a stockpile of usable fibres.

-- Sooty and sweep --

When you're ready for bed and the fire is still glowing in the hearth, douse the flames with a little salt to make the fire burn out more quickly (without making the fireplace damp). This way not only will there be less soot in the morning than if the fire had been left to smoulder for hours, but the salt also makes it easier to sweep up.

-- Grease lightening --

If you have grease stains on the carpet, mix up one part salt to four parts methylated spirits. Rub the mixture hard on the soiled area to clear it up.

-- Fizzled out --

Just as it can help clear your head in the morning, a few tablets of Alka-Seltzer are an effective way to clean stubborn stains from your coffee maker. Fill the percolator with water and drop in some Alka-Seltzer tablets. When they've dissolved, run the coffee-making cycle a few times and rinse thoroughly to get rid of any residue. The same trick should also work with mucky vases, crockery and thermoses.

-- Small mercies --

By the time you've smuggled them home in your suitcase those miniature toiletries that your hotel so nicely provided during your stay have travelled miles — only to be used once and then thrown away. Instead, put the little bottles to good use as lunch box coolers. Wash them out, fill them with water and freeze them to keep your sandwiches fresh all morning.

-- Spokes man --

There may well come a time in your life when you desperately need a kebab skewer but all you have to your name is a bicycle wheel. In such a situation you will be happy to discover that by filing down the ends of the spokes into points, your barbecue prayers will be answered. Need a spike but got no spokes? Take a pencil sharpener to a disposable wooden chopstick instead.

-- Round round baby --

A dead washing machine is a mine of new treasures, especially if it passes away in the summer: with rubber and plastic components removed, the metal drum makes a superb barbecue. If arranged in the right manner it can still be spun around, hot coals and all, which helps to fan the flames and get the party started. In cold weather, of course, it can make an equally effective salad spinner. Don't forget to salvage the glass door for something to serve the salad in, too.

-- Got it taped --

For want of a clothes brush to remove pet hair from upholstery or curtains, try a wad of adhesive tape instead. While masking tape is great for pet hair and lint (wrap it around your hand and pat the item), duct tape is so strong it can work wonders to get the bobbles off wool cushions.

-- Soft landing --

Fold an old dishcloth and place it at the bottom of the sink before washing delicate glass or china items, in case you accidentally drop anything.

-- Pressing issues --

The floor, for anyone who has tried, does not make a great ironing board. Carpet hairs get all over the clothes, and even with a towel over a wooden floor, the garment moves around and get soggy from the steam very quickly. If you're in an emergency situation where your pressed for time and need to press your shirt even faster, make a makeshift solution using a newspaper wrapped inside a pillow case.

&made
Ceramic Putty
Instead of discarding crockery
when it is broken or cracked,
design duo &made suggests
displaying its flaws for all to
see. Damaged plates, vases
and bowls can be fixed using
brightly coloured Ceramic
Putty, transforming the
fractures into new patterns
and decorative features.

-- Wash bags --

What does one do for drainage when all the colanders have been made into lampshades and hanging baskets? One uses a clean plastic bag. Although not so great for draining hot foods such as pasta, a plastic bag with a few holes punched in the bottom is ideal for washing vegetables.

-- Well red --

Some people swear that pouring white wine over a red-wine spillage is the best way to save a carpet at a party. It's a sensible option: white wine is usually the nearest thing to hand, and it's imperative to act while the spillage is still wet. The white wine will dilute the pigment and keep the red wine from drying while you go and fetch clean water, a sponge and some salt. After cleaning the area with water, sprinkle the salt over the whole mess and leave it for twenty minutes before vacuuming it all up.

-- Crumby idea --

A strange and somewhat questionable tip from bygone days: use stale bread to clean wallpaper. First sweep off the dust, then cut off a large crust and use it to wipe down the wall from top to bottom. You might be better off using the bread to feed the ducks, but it's your call.

-- Hit the headlines --

Newspaper is much better than a sponge or cloth for cleaning glass. Just tear it into strips of about 5 cm in width, ball them up and use as you would a paper towel. The paper leaves very little lint compared to paper towels, as newsprint is much more rigid and the fibres won't separate. There's no fear of the ink coming off as it is absorbed by the wet paper, and on a highly polished surface like glass there is nothing for the ink to stick to.

-- Snow better way --

As those who live in cold climates will know, to get a rug clean put
it out in the snow on a cold, dry, snowy day and leave it until frozen
before whacking the exposed surface with a broom or carpet beater
Pick it up, shake it out, turn it over and repeat, and then leave it a little
longer for sublimation to occur naturally. Finally brush off any snow
carefully before bringing the rug back into the house.

-- Take it to the wax --

Shoe polish is made of the same stuff as furniture polish – wax – and
can therefore be used to to touch up small nicks or scratches. The
main difference is that it's had colour added, so match the shade
carefully before applying it to your best mahogany. Warm polish works
best, so if you store the shoe polish in a cold place like a cellar, let it
get to room temperature before using.

-- Wipe and ready --

Make your own dustless dusters by soaking clean rags in a solution
of water and lemon oil (one part lemon oil in about twenty parts hot
water). Wring the cloths out and then hang them somewhere cool
and dry for twenty-four hours. Once the dusters have been used,
they can be washed as usual in the machine and treated again.

--Eggs benefit --

Wash and crush some eggshells and swill them around
in a little water to clean items such as mucky vases,
coffee jugs or wine decanters.

Design example
Jane ní Dhulchaointigh
SUGRU

SUGRU has been devised to enable people to reuse and fix hundreds of everyday items by crafting new handles and controls for them. A range of silicone-based materials that set at room temperature, SUGRU is a putty-like substance that can be formed into any required shape before hardening to a very tough, rubber-like, finished product. It was invented by Irish designer Jane ní Dhulchaointigh during her studies at the Royal College of Art in 2004.

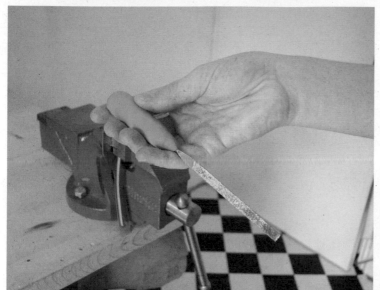

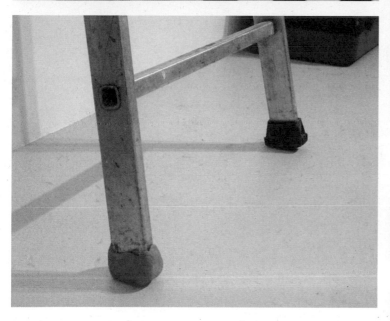

-- Sweet solution --
Sugar is very effective in eliminating tea stains from linen. After a particularly wild and reckless tea party, take the tablecloth and immerse it in a strong solution of sugar and water (add enough sugar that it won't completely dissolve), before rinsing and washing as usual.

-- For everything there is a season --
Sugar and salt are not the only seasonings to moonlight as cleaning agents. A teaspoon of peppercorns, added to a washload, will keep bright colours from fading, as well as reducing the risk that the dye will run into other garments.

-- Drain stops play --

A halved tennis ball makes as a small suction-cup device that can be used on those tricky occasions when a sink plunger isn't immediately to hand (but a tennis ball is). Position the ball over the drain, cut-side down, and press repeatedly to loosen the obstruction.

-- Polish all star --
A homemade metal polish for use on brass, bronze, copper and pewter can be mixed using equal parts flour, salt and white vinegar. Combine the salt and flour in a small bowl before adding the vinegar to make a thick paste. Smear onto the metal with a damp cloth and rub gently. Let the polish dry (this will take about an hour), rinse well with warm water and buff to a high shine. (This polish is not suitable for silver.)

-- Weight in line --

Fill old bottles with sand and rocks and use as a collection of weights. Small containers can work well as kitchen weights, larger ones are good for home fitness. The contents can be quite imaginative: ballbearings, feathers or coloured water, depending on whether you'd also like your weights to look lovely.

-- No more tears --

Vegetables are important weapon in the kitchen arsenal and can be put to good use in situations beyond your basic food fight. Onions, for example, should always be called into action against rust: plunge a rusty old kitchen knife or pair of scissors into a raw onion a few times and it ought to emerge good as new.

-- Spud, sweat and tears --

If you have grease marks on your finest silk upholstery, you'd better serve potatoes for dinner, because there's nothing better for getting out the marks than potato water mixed with a little ammonia. (A tablespoon of ammonia should be enough for a medium-sized pan of potato water.) Sponge away the stain with the mixture, fold the fabric while it's still damp, and press with a cool iron.

-- Flies to the moon --

Flies are a nuisance, but if you have a plastic litre bottle to hand they needn't be. Cut the top off the bottle about a third of the way down, invert the top and position it over the base as if it were a funnel. Place a bait in the bottom half - meat, honey, rotting fruit, old wine and dog poo are all serviceable options, depending on how close you might need to stand to the trap. Tape the two parts of the bottle together, hang the device from a tree or leave it in a prominent fly-infested position, and wait for your trap to reap its results as the flies enter through the funnel and can't escape. As a short cut you can also use a normal kitchen funnel and a wine bottle, or a cone of paper and a jam-jar.

Setting up

All it really takes to become a Remaker is a little common sense, a little planning, and, of course, this book. Here are some tips to help you on your way.

A common misconception about embracing the Remake lifestyle is that you have to become what is known as 'a hoarder'. This is simply not true. Excessive stockpiling and collecting are actually rather unfashionable – they clash with the ideal of sophisticated, modern living; where minimal lines and pared-down design are key. Clutter is not, generally speaking, considered a good look. Collecting can also be difficult if you happen to live in a small apartment and don't have the luxury of a 'junk room' in which to keep all those things that might, one day, come in handy.

    In practice, keeping track of odds and ends is only as messy as you make it. You don't need to keep a perpetual store of junk anywhere. If you can't see a use for an item straight away, chances are you never will; all it will do it gather dust, rust and acquire a slightly depressing air. Either (re)use the object immediately, or loose it – it's as simple as that. If you are short on inspiration, then this book is the perfect place to start.

    That said, certain items ARE worth saving, as they can be useful in so many ways. These include:

_ Jam jars
_ Tupperware
_ Tyres and inner-tubes
_ Spare fabric
_ Paper scraps
_ Boxes
_ Plastic bags
_ Wine corks

If you find yourself overflowing with any of the above, then it's probably time to stop collecting (and start recycling) until you find a use.

    When you are fully stocked and ready to repurpose, the next thing you will need is the redoubtable remaker's toolbox. Its advisable to have all the standard gadgets to hand, and a few extra supplies (including a sewing kit) up your sleeve.

Traditional toolbox items:
_ Hammer and nails
_ Selection of screws and screwdrivers
_ Selection of wallplugs
_ Nuts and bolts
_ Saws
_ Craft knife, utility knife or scalpel
_ Spirit level
_ Adjustable wrench
_ C-clamp
_ Electrical tape or duct tape (there's a school of thought that if you can't fix it with this, you just haven't used enough)
_ Masking tape
_ Selection of sandpaper in different grades
_ Electric drill
_ Tape measure
_ Wood glue and craft glue
_ Glue gun and hot glue sticks

A sewing kit will include:
_ Selection of threads and yarns
_ Needles (sewing, embroidery and upholstery)
_ Ribbon
_ Scissors
_ Buttons

- Hooks and eyes and other fastenings
- Safety pins and sewing pins
- Thimble (optional)
- Darning mushroom (optional, but brilliant)
- Sewing machine (will speed up most jobs)

Useful extra supplies to have around:
- Selection of paints (spray paints, emulsions, glass paint etc)
- Paint trays and brushes
- Pens and pencils
- Magnets
- Hooks
- String and strong cord
- Rope
- Selection of cables and wires
- Varnish
- Vinyl sheeting
- Double-sided sticky tape (a very useful, tidy, glue alternative)
- Glass-cutting kit
- Straps (cable straps, luggage straps, old belts etc...)
- Rubber bands
- Skewers
- Double-ended screws (vital when making and attaching knobs)
- Glitter (for decorating)
- Children (for doing the decorating)
- Paper shredder (or just ask the child)
- Etching cream for decorating (yes, it exists – use it on glass for a sandblasted effect)
- Rubber gloves
- Sticky labels
- Tea and cake (optional, but recommended)

The tips and instructions in this book are intended as inspiration. The nature of this way of working means that the materials, tools and outcomes of every project are likely to differ hugely depending on what you have to hand. This book will hopefully help you to find new uses for everyday things, but how you get from one thing to the other will be largely up to your own ingenuity. Use your imagination and experiment, but also remember to use your nous, and play safely.

A

Afroditi Krassa Ltd
Unit 37
DRCA Business Centre
Charlotte Despard Avenue
London SW11 5HD, UK
T: +44 (0) 20 7627 3463
www.afroditi.com

AMPLIFIER
Florian Kremb
Studio 34
Sara Lane Studios
60 Stanway Street
London N1 6RH, UK
T: +44 (0) 7941 419962
www.myamplifier.co.uk

Anarchitect
6 St Margarets House
21 Old Ford Road
London E2 9PL, UK
T: +44 (0) 20 8880 7666
www.
weareanarchitect.com

Claudia Araujo
r. Pelotas, 367
CEP 04012-001
São Paulo
Brazil
T: +55 11 5539 7429
www.claudiaaraujo.com.br

Majid Asif
27 Halifax Road
Shirley
Solihull B90 2BS, UK
T: +44 (0) 79 4456 2463
www.masifdesigns.com

Jorre van Ast
35 Bentley Road
N1 4BY London, UK
T: +44 (0) 20 8880 0690
www.jorrevanast.com

B

Maarten Baas
Studio Baas & Den
Herder BV
Eindhovenseweg 102c
5582 HW Waalre
The Netherlands
T: +31 6 2450 2082
www.maartenbaas.com

Gijs Bakker
Keizersgracht 518
1017 EK
Amsterdam
The Netherlands
www.gijsbakker.com

Tom Ballhatchet
13 Myddleton Avenue
London N4 2FA, UK
T: +44 (0) 77 9569 2704
www.tomballhatchet.com

**Huda Baroudi and
Maria Hubri**
Al Saabah Collection
Chatham/Mosaic Building
Design Miami District
155 NE 40th Street
Suite #101, Miami
FL 33137, USA
www.
alsabahcollection.com

Marina Bautier
14 rue Raphaëla
Brussels 1070, Belgium
T: +32 (0) 2520 0319
www.
lamaisondemarina.com

Denise Bird
Fine Fayre
60 Drake Avenue
Worcester WR2 5RZ, UK
T: +44 (0) 1905 425480
www.finefayre.co.uk/
denisebirdwoventextiles

Tord Boontje
La Cour
Route de Graix
42220 Bourg-argental
France
T: +33 4 7739 6604
www.tordboontje.com

Rita Botelho
Rua do Trevo 4
Quinta do Rouxinol
2855-206 Corroios
Portugal
T: +351 2 1254 5389
www.ritabotelho.com

Boym Partners Inc.
131 Varick Street
Room 915
New York, NY 10013
USA
T: +1 212 807 8210
www.boym.com

Laurence Brabant
134 rue des Couronnes
75020 Paris, France
T: +33 (0) 1 4036 1148
www.
laurencebrabant.com

Brave Space Design
449 Troutman St
Studio 2A
Brooklyn NY 11237, USA
T: +1 718 417 3180
www.
bravespacedesign.com

Abigail Brown
Textile artist and illustrator
Studio E2R Cockpit Arts
Cockpit Yard Northington
Street
London WC1N 2NP, UK
www.abigail-brown.co.uk

Tim Brown
SomeRightsReserved
T: +44 (0) 20 7502 0408
www.kith-kin.co.uk/shop/
idea

C

**Fernando and
Humberto Capana**
www.campanas.com.br

Maarten De Ceulaer
Interior-Industrial Designer
Vanderschrickstraat 59
1060 Brussels, Belgium
T: +32 (0) 49 489 4730
www.
maartendeceulaer.com

Alabama Chanin
462 Lane Drive
Florence
Alabama 35630, USA
T: +1 256 760 1090
www.alabamachanin.com

Checkland Kindleysides
Charnwood, Cossington
Leicestershire LE7 4UZ
UK
T: +44 (0) 1162 644700
www.checkland
kindleysides.com

Roman Christov
QUBUS design
Ramova 3
Praha 1 110 00
Czech Republic
T: +420 222 313 151
www.qubus.cz

Paul Cocksedge
2A Brenthouse Road
Soloman's Yard
London E9 6QG, UK
T: +44 (0) 208 985 0907
www.paulcocksedge.co.uk

Brent Comber
1657 Columbia Street
North Vancouver, BC
V7J 1A5, Canada
T: +1 604 980 4467
www.brentcomber.com

**Committee Gallop
Workshop**
198 Deptford High Street
London SE8 3PR, UK
T: +44 (0)20 8694 8601
www.gallop.co.uk

Complett
Jan Korbes
Kepplerstraat 304
2562vx Den Haag
The Netherlands
T: +31 615094323
www.refunc.nl

Creative Paper Wales
Broniestyn House
Trecynon, Aberdare
Mid Glamorgan
South Wales
CF44 8EF, UK
T: +44 (0)1685 872453
www.CreativePaperWales.
co.uk

**Michael Cross and Julie
Mathias**
WOKmedia
London Production
2 Leswin Place, Unit HQ
London N16 7NJ, UK
www.wokmedia.com

Shanghai Production
WOKmedia
Rujin Road 500 (South)
Shanghai
www.wokmedia.com

Margaret Cusack
124 Hoyt Street in Boerum
Hill Brooklyn
New York 11217-2215
USA
T: +1 718 2370145
www.
MargaretCusack.com

D

Jane ní Dhulchaointigh
FORMEROL® / SUGRU
FormFormForm Ltd 13
Hague Street,
London E2 6HN, UK
T: +44 (0) 20 7739 9446
www.formformform.com

Droog Press
Staalstraat 7a
1011 JJ Amsterdam
The Netherlands
T: +31 (0)20 523 5050
www.droog.com

E

Piet Hein Eek
Eek & Ruijgrok BV
Nuenenseweg 167
5667 KP Geldrop
The Netherlands
T: 040-2856610
www.pietheineek.nl

Emiliana Design Studio
Ana Mir and Emili Padrós
Aribau 230-240, 8° N
08006 Barcelona
Spain
T: +34 93 414 34 80
www.emilianadesign.com

Estudio en Pieza
Belmonte de Tajo
28019 Madrid
Spain
T: +34 911968571
www.enpieza.com

Ellie Evans
21 Woodside Denby Dale
Huddersfield
West Yorkshire HD8 8QX
UK
T: +44 (0)7745 528609
www.ellie-evans.co.uk

F

Jens Fager
A&D
Körsbärsvägen 9
11423 Stockholm
Sweden
T: +46 73 7272748
www.jensfager.se

Lucy Fergus
Re-Silicone
Studio 200, Cockpit Arts
18-22 Creekside, Deptford
London SE8 3DZ, UK
T: 07815 089 121
www.re-silicone.co.uk

Leo Fitzmaurice
T: +44 (0)7939 761640

Freitag
Hardstrasse 219/L
CH - 8005 Zürich
Switzerland
T: +41 (0)43 210 33 11
www.freitag.ch

G

Martino Gamper
Gamper Ltd.
65 Marlborough Avenue
E84JR London, UK
T: +44 (0)798 951 2239
www.gampermartino.com

David Gardner
T: 07929840206
www.davidgardener.co.uk

Kate Goldsworthy
www.kategoldsworthy.
co.uk

Graypants Inc.
1506 11th Avenue
Seattle, WA 98122
USA
T: 2064203912
www.graypants.com

Will Gurley
T: US- +1 505 333 4105
DK- +45 29 87 12 34
UK- +44 020 8123 6100
www.willgurley.com

H

Catherine Hammerton
Printed & Embroidered
Textiles
Studio E14, Cockpit Arts
Cockpit Yard
Northington Street
London WC1N 2NP, UK
T:+ 44 (0) 2076 038 851
www.
catherinehammerton.com

Ineke Hans
Dijkstraat 105
6828JS
Arnheim
The Netherlands
T: +31 (0) 263893892
www.inekehans.com

Stuart Haygarth
33 Dunloe Street
London E2 8JR, UK
T: +44 (0) 20 7503 4142
www.stuarthaygarth.com

Simon Heijdens
17 Sunbury Workshops
Swanfield Street
London E2 7LF, UK
T: +44 (0)78 5346 4303
www.simonheijdens.com

Heineken N.V.
Media relations
Tweede
Weteringplantsoen 21
1017 ZD Amsterdam
The Netherlands
T: +31 (0)20 5239 355
www.
heinekeninternational.com

Alex Hellum
64 Birch Green
Hertford, Herts
SG14 2LU, UK
T: +44 (0)1992 550 021
www.alexhellum.com

Amy Hunting
Flat C, 17-19 Mare Street
London E8 4RS, UK
T: +44 7501 821 218
www.amyhunting.com

J

Peter van der Jagt
Sumatrakade 275
1019PK Amsterdam
The Netherlands
T: +31 (0) 20 4198731
www.petervanderjagt.com

Anneke Jakobs
Haverstaadt 5 Bis
3511 NA, Utrecht
The Netherlands
www.annekejakobs.com

**JAM, The Art of
Branding**
103 The Timber Yard
Drysdale Street
London N1 6ND, UK
T. +44 (0) 20 7739 6600
www.jamdesign.co.uk

Junktion Workshop
Gurit Magen
Junktion studio
Rosh Pina st. 22/9
Tel Aviv 66026, Israel
T: +972 52 3637104
www.junktion.co.il

K

Kako.ko Design Studio
Dositejeva 30a
11000 Belgrade, Serbia
T: +381 11262 4001
www.kako-ko.com

Johanna Keimeyer
Motzstr.5
10777 Berlin, Germany
T: +49 179 35 91 657
www.keimeyer.com

Sante Kim
T: +82 (0)10 4143 3075
www.santekim.com

Diaz Kleefstra
Studio Kleefstra
P.O. Box 11253G
Amsterdam
The Netherlands
T: +31 653 535503
www.studiokleefstra.nl

Jan Körbes
Tyre Furniture
Kepplerstraat 304
2562vx den haag
The Netherlands
T: +316 1509 4323
www.refunc.nl

Kyouei Design
1326-15 Kusanagi
Shimizu-ku
Shizuoka City
Shizuoka 424-0886
Japan
www.kyouei-ltd.co.jp

L

Andreas Linzner
Marktstrasse 6
20357 Hamburg
Germany
T: +49 40 433435
www.andreaslinzner.com

**London Transport
Museum**
39 Wellington Street,
Covent Garden
London WC2E 7BB, UK
T: +44 (0)20 7379 6344
www.ltmuseum.co.uk

Lost and Found
Becky Oldfield
Studio 108, Cockpit Arts
18-22 Creekside, Deptford
London SE8 3DZ, UK
T: 07958 324038
www.
lostandfounddesign.co.uk

Loyal Loot Collective
75 Gainsborough Ave
St. Albert, Alberta
T8N 1Z5, Canada
T: +1 780 916 9148
www.loyalloot.com

Seija Lukkala
Globe Hope Tld.
Harjutie 14
FIN 03100 Nummela
Finland
T: +35892238150
www.globehope.com

Greg Lynn
Form
1817 Lincoln Boulevard
Venice CA 90291, USA
T: 310.821.2629
www.glform.com

M

&Made
Studio 214
18-22 Creekside, Deptford
London, SE8 3DZ, UK
T: + 44 (0)79 1617 0293
www.and-made.com

Michael Marriott
Unit F2
2-4 Southgate Road
London N1 3JJ, UK
www.michaelmarriott.com

Barley Massey
Fabrications
7 Broadway Market
Hackney
London E8 4PH, UK
T: 020 7275 8043
M: 07968 424 808
www.fabrications1.co.uk

Franz Maurer
Showroom: A-1030 Wien,
Rechte Bahngasse 40
Studio: A-3874
Haugschlag 12, Vienna
Austria
M: +43-699-10 101 102
T: +43-1-512 10 30
www.fmaurer.com

**Maybe Design
Studio Vienna**
Burggasse 7/8
A-1013 Vienna, Austria
T: +43 1 5332636
F: +43 15332665
www.maybeproduct.at

Maybe Design Studio
Istanbul
Akin Plaza K.3 Sisli
TR-34382 Istanbul
Turkey
T: +90 212 320 9561
F: +90 212 320 9562

Ryan McElhinney
72 Blackfriars Road
Waterloo
London SE1 8HA, UK
T: +44 (0)2079285466
www.ryanmcelhinney.com

Jo Meesters
Kanaalstraat 4
5611 CT, Eindhoven
The Netherlands
T. +31 (0) 65 422 31 88
www.jomeesters.nl

Menimal
Carlos Francisco Cantú
Cavada
Monterrey, NM, USA
T: +52 045 (81) 16900160
www.fcocantu.
carbonmade.com

M:ome
www.mome.org/

Jasper Morrison
2b Kingsland Road
London E3 8DA, UK
www.jaspermorrison.com

Nicolas Le Moigne
17, Avenue de Jurigoz
CH-1006 Lausanne
Switzerland
www.
nicholaslemoigne.com

Muji
James Lawless
Press Officer MUJI (UK)
Press Office
1 Carnaby Street
London 1F 7DX, UK
T: +44 (0)207 221 9360

Zoe Murphy
Studio 4
The Pie Factory
9 Broad Street
Margate, Kent
CT9 1EW, UK
T: 07780574314
www.zoemurphy.com

N

Heath Nash
T: +27 21 447 5757

Nendo
2-2-16-5F Shimomeguro
Meguro-ku
Tokyo 153-0064, Japan
T: +81-(0)3-6661-3750
www.nendo.jp

Emma Neuberg
www.emmaneuberg.
blogspot.com

Elisabeth Nossen
Elisabeth N. Ellefsen
Nygaardsgaten 2A
N-5015 Bergen, Norway
T: +47 99 70 08 63
www.rebelledesign.
blogspot.com

O
Od-Do Arhitekti
Aleksinackih Rudara 31
Belgrade, Serbia
T: +38 1606906069
www.od-do.com

P
Marjie van der Park
Terwestenstraat 49
5613 HH Eindhoven
The Netherlands
T: +31 (0)6 24184787
www.
hmarijevanderpark.nl

Pervisioni
Paul Kogelnig,
Gabriel Heusser
Institut für Visionen
& Co KG
Mariahilferstrasse 45
1060 Wien, Austria
T: +43 (0)699 14085911
www.pervisioni.com

Jens Praet
via Chiantigiana 4
50020 Panzano, Chianti
Italy
T: +39 334 3091223
www.jenspraet.com

R
Tal R.
Fritz Hansen
Allerødvej 8
3450 Allerød, Denmark
T: +45 4817 2300
www.fritzhansen.com

Raw Nerve Ltd
B109, Faircharm Studios
Creekside
London SE8 3DX, UK
T: +44 (0)20 8692 4343
www.raw-nerve.co.uk

Tejo Remy
Uraniumweg 17
3542 AK, Utrecht
The Netherlands
T: +31 (0)302944945
www.remyveenhuizen.nl

Rotor
Maarten Gielen
Laekensestraat 101
1000 Brussel, Belgium
T: +32 485 875763
www.rotordb.org

Adrien Rovero Studio
Chemin des Roses 11
CH-1020 Renens
Switzerland
T: +41 (0)21 634 34 35
www.adrienrovero.com

Galya Rosenfeld
12 Rabbi Meir Street
Tel-Aviv, 65605, Israel
T: +972 (0) 50-259-4627
www.gaylarosenfeld.com

Karen Ryan
www.bykarenryan.co.uk

S
Alyce Santoro
P.O. Box 176
Fort Davis, Texas 79734
USA
www.alycesantoro.com
www.sonicfabric.com

Scrapile
70 North 6th Street
Brooklyn
New York 11211, USA
T: +1 917 826 3141
www.scrapile.com

Sergio Silva
196 Clinton Ave A44
Brooklyn, NY 11205, USA
T: +1 917 841 7075
www.sergiosilva.us

Sprout Design Ltd.
1 Bermondsey Square
London SE1 3UN, UK
T: +44 (0)20 7645 3790
www.sproutdesign.co.uk

Stanker Design
Motxo Design
F. Royer
4 Rue P. Mendès France
34830 Clapiers, France
T: +33 (0)681644740
http://stanker.design.
free.fr

Studio Mama
21-23 Voss Street
E2 6JE London, UK
T: +44 (0)20 7033 0408
www.studiomama.com

Studio Oooms
Gagelstraat 6a, ingang C
5611 BH Eindhoven
The Netherlands
T: +31 (0)40 29 38 326
www.oooms.nl

Studio Stallinga
Silodam 1 D
1013 AL Amsterdam
Netherlands
T: +31 (0)20 420 0876
www.stallinga.nl

Greetje van Tiem
Startumsedijk 18X
5611 ND, Eindhoven
The Netherlands
T: +31 (0)65 3260222
www.greetjevantiem.nl

T

Ting
16 Chelsea Farmers
Market
Sydney Street
London SW3 6NP, UK
T: +44 (0) 20 7751 4424
www.tinglondon.com

U

Uhuru Design
160 Van Brunt Street
Brooklyn NY, 11231
USA
T: +1 718 855 6519
www.uhurudesign.com
www.uhurudesign.com

V

Maxim Velcovsky
QUBUS design
Ramova 3
Praha 1, 110 00
Czech Republic
T: +42 (0)222 313 151
www.qubus.cz

Studio Verissimo
www.studioverissimo.net

Elmo Vermijs
Oude Haagseweg 63-1B
1066 DC Amsterdam
The Netherlands
T: +31 (0)6 435832911
www.elmovermijs.com

Clara Vuletich
Heafford & Hall
7 Prescott Place
London SW4 6BS, UK
T: +44 (0)7733 072 337
www.claravuletich.com
www.loveandthrift.com

W

Katherine Wardropper
Studio 100
Cockpit Arts Deptford
18-22 Creekside
Deptford
London SE8 3DZ, UK
T: +44 (0) 776 259 3363
www.
katherinewardropper.com

Silke Wawro
Volksware
Koburgerstr. 95
51103 Cologne
Germany
T: +49 173 4474416
web: www.volksware.nl

WEmake
Jason Allcorn and
Sarah Johnson
1 Summit way
Crystal Palace
London SE19 2PU, UK
T: +44 (0)7962 108782
www.wemake.co.uk

Dominic Wilcox
www.dominicwilcox.com

Frank Willems
Studio Frank Willems
Lucas Gasselstraat 7A
5611 ST Eindhoven
The Netherlands
T: +31 (0)6 283 405 98

Donna Wilson
BJ House 12
Third floor
10-14 Hollybush Gardens
London E2 9QP, UK
T: +44 (0)20 7749 0768
www.donnawilson.com

Emma Woffenden
Marsden Woo Gallery
17-18 Great Sutton Street
London EC1V 0DN, UK
T: +44 (0)20 7336 6396
www.bmgallery.co.uk

Z

Dmitry Zagga
www.zagga.org

**Zo_Loft Architecture
& Design s.r.l.**
Andrea Cingoli
Paolo Emilio Bellisario
Francesca Fontana
Cristian Cellini
Via Piave 91, 65100
Pescara, Italy
T: +39 3381931673
www.zo-loft.com

Books:

Arkhipov, V.,
Home-Made:
Contemporary Russian
Folk Artifacts,
FUEL Publishing,
2006

Berger, S., and G.
Hawthorne,
Readymade: How to Make
(Almost) Everything,
Clarkson Potter,
2005

Dixon, T.,
Rethink,
Conran Octopus,
2000

Gibson, J. J.,
The Theory of Affordances
in *Perceiving, Acting and*
Knowing,
Shaw, R., and J. Bransford
(eds.), Hillsdale,
1977

Hanaor, Z., and V.
Woodcock,
Making Stuff: An
Alternative Craft Book,
Black Dog Publishing,
2006

Jencks, C., and N. S.
Jencks,
Adhocism,
Doubleday & Co.,
1972

Lupton, E.,
DIY: Design it Yourself,
Princeton Architectural,
Press,
2006

Norman, J.,
Make Do and Mend:
Keeping Family and
Home Afloat on War
Rations (Official WWII
Info Reproductions),
Michael O'Mara,
2007

Readers Digest
Association,
Extraordinary Uses
for Ordinary Things,
2005

Warner, M.,
Richard Wentworth,
Thames & Hudson,
1993

Magazines:

Make Magazine
Crafts Magazine
Design Week
Wallpaper
Metropolis
Dwell
Icon

Websites:

Instructables.com
Superuse.org
Treehugger.com
Dezeen.com
MarthaStewart.com
Apartmenttherapy.com
Inhabitat.com
Coolhunting.com
Wemakemoneynotart.com

Acknowledgments

Henrietta Thompson
would like to thank
(in no particular order):
Jubi, Simon, Alan,
Jacquie, Olivia, Angus,
Neal, Emmi, Charlie,
Tim, Adala, Andrew, Jo,
Joey, Jess, Simon J,
Simon W, Jon H, all at
Thames & Hudson and
Katie The Cat.

Neal Whittington
would like to thank Mum,
Dad and Mark.

Key:

a = above
b = below
c = centre
l = left
r = right

6bl Knotted Chair for Droog by Marcel Wanders, photo Robaard/ Theuwkens, styling by Marjo Kranenbourg, CMK

7ar Tree-Trunk Bench for Droog by Jurgen Bey, photo Gerard van Hees

7br Set Up Shades for Droog by Marcel Wanders, photo Robaard/ Theuwkens, styling by Marjo Kranenbourg, CMK

9ar, **br** Kokon Furniture by Jurgen Bey

10a, b; 11a, b Leo Fitzmaurice

15a Francisco Cantú

16–17 Angus Mill

18a NEMECHEK photography studio, Israel

18bl Copyright © Rotor

20al Morrison Studio, Jasper Morrison Ltd. Flower Pot Table produced by Cappellini

20bl Peter Guenzel, Jasper Morrison Ltd., Crate produced by Established & Sons

25al, ar Tom Ballhatchet

25bl Uhuru

26al, bl designed by Fernando and Humberto Campana and produced by Estudio Campana 2002, photo Luiz Calazans

27al Rag Chair for Droog by Tejo Remy, photo Robaard/Theuwkens, styling by Marjo Kranenbourg, CMK

27ar Rag Chair for Droog by Tejo Remy, photo Gerard van Hees

29al Design Maarten Baas, photo Maarten van Houten

31a www.wemake.co.uk

31bl Raef Grohne

32b Jonathan Junker

33a, b Scrapile Studio

35a, bl, bc, br Masayuki Hayashi

38al, ar, b © Motxo Design 2008

39bl MUUTO

40a, bl, br photo Tomas Leach

41a, b Xavier Padrós

46a, b Jan Korbes/ REFUNC.NL

46 Roma Levin

47 a, bl, br Fracture Furniture by Ineke Hans for Cappellini

48al, ar, b Serge Hagemeier

50al, ar, b © Stine Raarup

51a Life Is Suite – www.lifeissuite.co.uk

51b Majid Asif

57br courtesy of Alessi

79ar Foto Zechany, Vienna

79br Jo Meesters

80 One Day Paper Waste for Droog by Jens Praet, photo Bas Helders

81ar, br, l One Day Paper Waste for Droog by Jens Praet, photo Gerard van Hees

82 photo Olivier Pasqual

89ar photo David Cripps

101a photo Bradley Walker

101bl Pelle Crepin

103a, c NEMECHEK photography studio, Israel

111 photo Connect Architecture

113a, b designed by Maarten de Ceulaer and Julien van Havere

114 Dian Simpson

115a Emiliana Design

119l Ricardo João Faria

124, 125al, ac, ar, bl, br photo Angela Moore

128 TIDE (2004), photo Stuart Haygarth

129a MILLENIUM, photo Stuart Haygarth

129bl SPECTACLE (2006), photo Stuart Haygarth

138a, bl, br; 139a, bl, br David Southwood

142l, ar, cr, br David Gardner

143l, r © Richard Brine

148a, b NEMECHEK photography studio, Israel

158 photo Full Focus

158ar Kate Goldsworthy

158br styling Kate Parkin, photo Lucy Pope

163 artist/designer: Margaret Cusack, client: Vanity Fair Magazine, art director: Julie Weiss, photographer: Michael Hnatov

164 Jo Meesters and Marielle Leenders

165al, ac, ar, b photo Rob Brodman

166a, ar, ac, br Muji

172a, b photo Tim Bjørn www.fritzhansen.com

173a, c, b Robert Rausch/ GAS Design Center

179a, c, b James Champion

180al, ac, ar, b TINGLONDON.COM

181al, ar, cl, cr, b Matthew Murphy (2008)

183a, b photo Julian Mock

184al, ar, bl, br London Transport Museum www.ltmuseum.co.uk

185a Destination Blinds, photo James Gardiner

185b photo Kevin Dutton

186al, ar, b Lucy Fergus

188l, cr, br; 189 Roberto Setton – São Paulo, Brazil

190al Vincent van Gurp

194a, b; 195a, c, b Arooj Hussein

197al, ar, c, b SCP

200br photo by the artist, © 2007, all rights reserved

201a, b Paul Schimweg, www.whitehall-photographie.de

203a, b Nina Merikallio

209a photo Michael Rathmayr

213a, b Xavier Nicostrate

218, 219a, b producer: Viceversa, photo: Anoush Abrar

220 Kyouei Design

224a, bl, br Sprout Design Ltd

226 Bottoms-Up doorbell for Droog by Peter van der Jagt, photo Gerard van Hees

232 Sante Kim

235al, ar, b Olga Telesh

239a, b Dishmop for Droog by Gijs Bakker, photo Gerard van Hees

243 Tom Ballhatchet

244 © Zo-loft Architecture & Design S r.l.

251r Roma Levin

254al, ar, b; 255al, bl, ar, cr, br © Form Form Form Ltd, 2009